Curri**CUlu**m Foc

Toys

Christine Moorcroft

HOPSCOTCH

A division of MA Education Ltd

Curriculum Focus series

History

Famous Events
Famous People
Invaders
Toys
Tudors

Geography

Islands and Seasides
The Local Area

Science

Ourselves
Animals, Plants and Habitats: Key Stage 1
Materials: Key Stage 1

Published by Hopscotch, A division of MA Education Ltd
St Jude's Church, Dulwich Road
Herne Hill, London SE24 0PB
Tel: 020 7738 5454

© 2009 MA Education Ltd

Written by Christine Moorcroft
Linked ICT activities by Michelle Singleton
Series design by Blade Communications
Illustrated by Martin Cater
Cover illustration by Susan Hutchison
Printed by Clintplan, Southam

Christine Moorcroft hereby asserts her moral right to be
identified as the author of this work in accordance with
the Copyright, Designs and Patents Act, 1988.

ISBN 978-1-90430-753-2

Contents

Cross-curricular links   4

Introduction   5

1 Our toys today   6

2 Old and new toys   14

3 A toy museum   22

4 Learning from pictures   29

5 Teddy bears   37

6 Models   47

7 Musical toys   55

8 Materials   63

Toys from the past: Roman to 1990s   71

Photocopiable word bank   84

References and resources   88

Cross-curricular links

Chapter	History SoW	Geography SoW	PSHE and Citizenship	Science SoW	Literacy framework	Numeracy framework	ICT SoW
1	Unit 1		2a 5c	1E	YR, W11 Y1, Term 1, W8 Y1, Term 2, W5, W10 Y1, Term 3, W8 Y2, Term 1, W5, W10	Y1, 2 Y1, 88 Y1, 90, 92 Y2, 91, 93	1E
2	Unit 1		2a 3d 5c 5e	1E	YR, W11 Y1, Term 1, W8, W9, W12; T14; S4 Y1, Term 2, W6, W10; S3 Y1, Term 3, W3, W4 Y2, Term 1, W5, W10	Y1, 82 Y1, 88	1B 1C
3	Unit 1	Unit 3	2a 5c	1C	YR, W11 Y1, Term 1, W8, W9, W12; T14; S4 Y1, Term 2, W6, W10; S3 Y1, Term 3, W3, W4 Y2, Term 1, W5, W10		1C
4	Unit 1	Unit 4	2a 3d 5c		YR, W11 Y1, Term 1, W12; T15 Y1, Term 2, W5; T25 Y1, Term 3, W3 Y2, Term 1, W5, W10		1C
5	Unit 1	Unit 5	2a 3d 5c 5e	1C	YR, W11 Y1, Term 1, W8, W12; T14; S4 Y1, Term 2, W10; S3 Y1, Term 3, W3 Y2, Term 1, W5, W10		1A 1C 1D
6	Unit 1		2a 5c	1C	YR, W11 Y1, Term 1, W8, W12; T14; S4 Y1, Term 2, W10; S3 Y1, Term 3, W3 Y2, Term 1, W5, W10	Y1, 88 Y2, 87, 89	1C 1F
7	Unit 1		2a 5c	1F	YR, W11 Y1, Term 1, T16; S4 Y1, Term 2, T22, T23, T25 Y2, Term 2, S5	Y1, 88	1C 1F
8	Unit 1		2a 5c	1C 2D	YR, W11 Y1, Term 1, S4 Y1, Term 2, T22, T23, T25		1B 1C

Introduction

Curriculum Focus: Toys helps to make history fun by giving you (especially those of you who are not history specialists) the support you need to plan stimulating and exciting lessons.

This book will help you to plan and teach a unit of work based on the QCA Exemplar Scheme of Work for History at Key Stage 1. Also, where appropriate, this book gives indications as to how the work can be linked with other areas of the curriculum.

The material in this book gives you a sound foundation from which to plan a unit of work for your classes. This includes:

- detailed **Teachers' notes** giving background information on each topic and/or the concept to be taught
- fully illustrated **Generic sheets** offering a wealth of reusable resource material
- a **Lesson plan** full of ideas for introducing and developing the lesson
- photocopiable and differentiated **Activity sheets** to support individual and group work
- a photocopiable word bank and pictures of toys from the past.

Any unit of work on toys will be enlivened by the use of photographs, coloured illustrations and real toys (both modern and old). Making a collection of old-fashioned toys can be time-consuming, but try friends of the school, children's families, jumble sales and car boot sales. The chapters are supported by a list of books and other printed materials, websites and addresses of museums from which pictures and other materials can be obtained (see **References and resources** on page 88 and 89). Indications are also given of the types of toys that the children's parents/carers, grandparents and older relations and friends might be able to lend to the school, or about which they might be willing to talk to the children.

There are also suggested questions for the children to ask people in order to elicit interesting and informative memories from their childhood, and ideas for helping the children to record what they find out. Local enthusiasts might be able to offer valuable help that will stimulate the children's interest and excitement.

Apart from Chapter 1, which should be used to introduce the work, you can select the chapters you want to use as a basis for a unit of work, and the chapters can be presented in any order.

The material in each chapter is designed to be used flexibly, and not necessarily consecutively with the whole class. It is recognised that many teachers of children of this age group prefer to organise their classes so that, after an initial teacher input, different groups work on different activities.

Curriculum Focus: Toys recognises that there will be different levels of attainment among the children and that their developing literacy skills will require different levels of support during individual and group work. To help you to provide activities suitable for children of different abilities, each chapter contains three photocopiable sheets based on the same material, but aimed at children of different levels of attainment. This enables the whole class to take part in a similar activity:

- Activity sheet 1 in each chapter is intended for lower-attaining children.
- Activity sheet 2 should be suitable for most children.
- Activity sheet 3 challenges the higher-attaining children.

CHAPTER 1

Our toys today

Children need to develop awareness of different kinds of modern toys in order to be able to compare them later with toys from the past.

Categories of modern toys

People and animals
This category of toys includes dolls, teddy bears, soft toys and model people and animals. Modern toys include many representing famous people, including pop stars, actors and characters from films, television programmes and books.

Models
This category of toys includes dolls' houses, replicas of other buildings, domestic and workplace equipment, vehicles, aeroplanes, spacecraft and boats. The rapid development of technology has given rise to innumerable model toys based on films, television programmes and books. For example, the *Star Wars* films all have an extensive range of model toys featuring spacecraft, alien buildings and landscapes.

Outdoor games and toys
This category of toys includes tents and play-houses, bicycles, cars, skates, scooters, swings, kites, games equipment and radio-controlled toys.

Indoor games and toys
This category of toys includes board games, electronic/computer games, torches, dressing-up outfits and radio-controlled toys.

Musical toys
The toys in this category include whistles, drums, guitars, keyboards and electronic instruments. More and more toy manufacturers are producing electronic-based instruments incorporating computer programs, allowing the user to compose their own music at the touch of a button.

Making and learning
This category includes paints, modelling materials and kits, as well as learning toys incorporating sophisticated computer programming.

Sources of illustrations

Retailers' brochures are useful sources of illustrations to cut out and glue on to cards for the children to sort. They can also be used ready sorted, since many brochures group toys in categories similar to those listed above.

Modern influences on toys

Toys today are influenced by factors such as books, films and television programmes. It is almost commonplace now for a range of merchandise (including toys) to be released at the same time as a major children's film.

Toys today also reflect everyday life. Many toys are replicas of the things adults use, such as domestic items (vacuum cleaners and washing machines), model cars (and other vehicles) made to look exactly like the real thing, dressing-up clothes, grooming kits and tool kits.

Today, children's choices of toys are strongly influenced by advertising, particularly during the period leading up to Christmas. Toys become 'must haves', and fads or crazes develop. Sometimes it seems that every child is playing with a particular toy and then, after a short time, it will be forgotten, only to be replaced by a new fad or craze. Examples of such fads include rollerblades, micro-light scooters, collectors' cards and stickers, and certain types of dolls and computer games.

Our toys today

History objectives (Unit 1)
- To describe the characteristics of new objects.
- To sort objects in different ways [develop skills of classifying toys].
- To use everyday words and phrases to describe an artefact.

Resources

- A collection of modern toys of different types:
  - **People and animals**: dolls, teddy bears, soft toys, model people and animals
  - **Models**: dolls' houses, replicas of other buildings, domestic and workplace equipment, vehicles, aeroplanes, spacecraft and boats
  - **Outdoor games and toys**: tents and play-houses, bicycles, cars, skates, scooters, swings and games equipment
  - **Indoor games and toys**: board games, electronic games, torches, dressing-up outfits
  - **Musical toys**: whistles, drums, electronic instruments
  - **Making and learning**: paints, modelling materials, kits
  - **Computer games**: adventures, simulations, battle games, competitive games and those which aid learning
- Pictures of toys from each of the above categories from brochures, catalogues and websites
- Scissors and glue
- Generic sheets 1 and 2 (pages 9 and 10)
- Activity sheets 1–3 (pages 11–13)

Starting points: *whole class*

Before the lesson ask the children to bring in a toy, preferably from a list you have made to ensure a variety. Write labels for the toys in the collection. Invite the children to come out and talk about the toy they have brought in. Ask them to name it and describe it, saying what colour it is and talking about parts of the toy and any shapes or patterns on it. They could talk about any important parts of the toy and say what they are for. They could also talk about when they play with it and with whom, and what they do when playing with it. Encourage the others to ask questions about the toy.

Questions to ask include:

- How do you use the toy?
- How does it work?
- Do you play with it alone? If not, who with?
- Do you play with it indoors or outdoors?
- Do you have any other toys like it?
- How are the toys alike?

After some of the children have described their toys, ask the class to think of a way in which to group the toys with others of the same kind. Ask them how the toys they have grouped together are alike. Introduce terms such as 'doll', 'soft toy', 'game', 'indoor game', 'computer game', 'outdoor game', 'outdoor toy', 'model', 'musical', 'for learning things' and 'for making things' and ask the children to point out a toy of each type.

Give the children copies of Generic sheets 1 and 2 and read the information with them. Ask them if they can recognise and name any of the toys in the pictures, and if they own any of these toys. Reinforce the idea that toys can be split into different types. Ask the children if they can think of any other kinds of toys.

Tell the children that they are going to cut out pictures of toys and sort them into sets of the same kind. Provide pairs of children with scissors and pictures of toys from each category. The children can choose how to group the toys. As they do so, talk about the groupings, which could be very simple: for example, 'computer games', 'dolls', 'play-house things' and 'cars' (introduce the word 'vehicle'). Help the children to label their sets.

Ask the children to think up sentences to describe their sets of toys, saying how they are similar and how they are different. For example, vehicles:

- 'They all have wheels.'
- 'Some are big and some are small.'
- 'There are cars, trucks, tractors and a fire engine.'

Group activities

Tell the children that they are now going to sort some pictures of toys into 'toy boxes' for different kinds of toys.

Activity sheet 1

This is for children who can sort familiar objects into sets using given criteria and can sort objects into two groups. With the children, read the headings on the toy boxes on the activity sheet and ask them to find a toy belonging in each box. They have to draw the toys in the correct boxes.

Activity sheet 2

This is for children who can sort familiar objects into sets using given criteria and can sort objects into four groups. With the children, read the headings on the toy boxes on the activity sheet and ask them to find a toy belonging in each box. Read the names of the toys with the children. They have to draw lines to link the toys to the correct toy boxes, then label the toys with the support of a word bank.

Activity sheet 3

This is for children who can sort familiar objects into sets using given criteria and can sort objects into four groups. They can also find objects which belong in different categories. With the children, read the captions under the toy boxes shown on the activity sheet and ask them to find a toy belonging in each box. They have to draw toys in each toy box. On the back of the sheet they have to draw a new toy box and some indoor toys in it.

Plenary session

Invite the children who completed Activity sheet 1 to show their pictures. Ask the class to say if each toy is in the correct toy box. The children who completed Activity sheet 2 could read aloud the headings of the toy boxes and say which toys they have linked to each one. Ask the others if they were right and if not, what was wrong. The children who completed Activity sheet 3 could say what toys they have drawn in their 'indoor games' toy box. Invite the children to suggest other toys to add to each toy box.

Ideas for support

Read the name of each toy on the Activity sheets and ask the children to find the same kind of toy (or a picture of it) in the classroom collection of toys. Point out the initial letters of the words and encourage the children to say the sounds of the letters.

Using Activity sheet 1, encourage the children to point to each toy, and ask them 'Is it an animal?' Ask them where it belongs if the answer is 'Yes' and where it belongs if the answer is 'No'. In the same way encourage the children working on Activity sheet 2 to look at each toy and then look at each toy box in turn to check if it belongs there.

Ideas for extension

Tell the children that they are going to learn about toys from the past. Ask them whom they might ask to find out about older toys.

Linked ICT activities

Ask the children about their favourite toys. What do they enjoy playing with, and why? On a flip chart list the categories: people and animals; models; outdoor games and toys; indoor games and toys; musical toys; making and learning; computer games. As the children talk about their favourites, decide with them which category the toy fits into and enter it on the chart. Then find out which is the most popular type of toy by counting the names in each category. Find out the most and the least popular type of toy.

Use the software *Counter for Windows* and select the program 'Counter'. (See References and resources on page 89.) Type in the information from the flip chart. Use the bar chart facility and the pie chart facility to answer questions based on the information displayed, such as 'How many children have a favourite toy that they play with outside?' Questions can be differentiated for the children's ability.

Create teaching resources by printing off the bar charts and pie charts. Use a word processing program to create your own worksheets based on the graphs. ('Look at the graph. Which is the favourite type of toy that children in our class like to play with?')

Talk to the children about how fast the computer can print the charts, compared with the time it would take you to draw them accurately.

Our toys today

There are many different kinds of toys.

People and animals

Models

Outdoor games and toys

Our toys today

There are many different kinds of toys.

Indoor games and toys

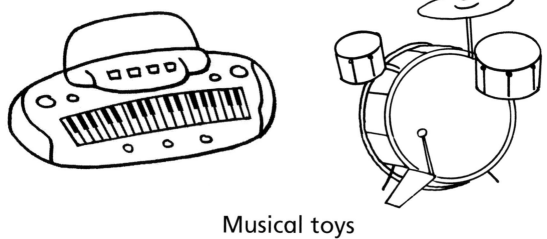

Musical toys

Making and learning

Name —————————————————

Our toys today

Which toys are animals?
Draw the toys in the toy boxes.

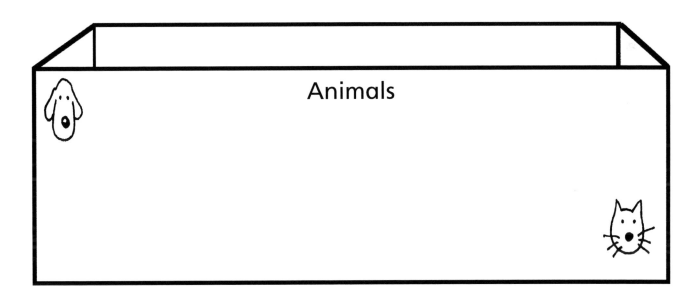

Animals

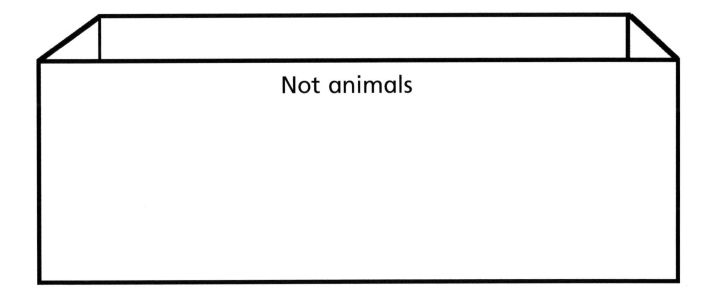

Not animals

Our toys today

Join the toys to the toy boxes. Then label each toy.
Use the word bank to help you.

Things to make

People toys

Musical toys

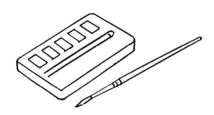

Animal toys

WORD BANK

doll	drum	keyboard	monkey	paints
	modelling clay	soldier		teddy

Our toys today

Draw toys in the toy boxes.
Label each toy.

Animal toys

Musical toys

People toys

Things to make

On the back of this sheet, draw a toy box with some indoor toys i

Old and new toys

The toys shown on Generic sheet 1 (see page 18) were available in the 1930s to 1950s; they could therefore be described to the children as 'toys your grandparents may have had'.

Dolls

During the Second World War most dolls made in the UK had bodies made from fabric and heads and limbs (or parts of limbs) made from pottery (ceramic), but there were also dolls made from 'composition' (a mixture of sawdust and glue or paper and glue) and rubber. Rag dolls were also popular.

After the Second World War, doll manufacturers began to use the newly available plastics. A popular doll from the 1950s was Tiny Tears, which had space inside her body for a water container connected to a small hole in the corner of each eye. Tiny Tears cried 'real tears' if her stomach was squeezed after she had been fed water from her feeding bottle.

There were also dolls made as models of real people (for instance, the child film star Shirley Temple) and fictional characters (for instance, Enid Blyton's Noddy).

Dolls' prams

Dolls' prams, like those of today, were smaller versions of real prams, as can be seen in the illustration of a 1950s' dolls' pram on Generic sheet 1. Many were produced by pram manufacturers, rather than by toy manufacturers. They were made from similar materials to real prams: coach-built metal frames with waterproof fabric hoods and aprons.

Toy cars and trucks

As with many toys, the main differences between modern model vehicles and those of the 1930s to 1950s are the styles (which mimic current real vehicles), the materials used and the technology involved. Sophisticated radio-controlled models have replaced the early battery-driven remote-controlled vehicles which became available in the 1960s, and manufacturers can now colour and

shape modern plastics to produce strong, realistic models, whereas early plastic vehicles were usually fragile and had painted designs which wore off.

Die-cast model cars were first made in 1914 (by the Dowst Manufacturing Company of Chicago, which produced a Model T Ford and went on to make the 'Tootsietoy' range). Britains and John Hill began to make them in the UK, but mainly to accompany their other die-cast models. Dinky model vehicles, manufactured from 1934, were popular through the 1950s and 1960s; these, like the ones made by Dowst, were small-scale replicas of the real vehicles of the time. Corgi models overtook Dinky in popularity, mainly because they were the first to have 'glass' in their windows.

On a smaller scale, Matchbox models, by Lesney of London (which made its first 'Matchbox Miniature' in 1947), were popular.

Wooden and tin plate cars were also available; they did not have the authentic look of the die-cast models, but many of the tin plate models had friction-powered engines ('push-and-go') and children used to enjoy racing them.

Indoor games

Some of the board games of the early twentieth century are still available, although their design has been modernised: for example, Ludo, Snakes and Ladders and Monopoly.

'Blow Football', introduced in the 1920s by Spear's, remained popular until the 1950s and even the 1960s. The 'pitch' could be any table, covered with a thick cloth (to stop the ball rolling too quickly); it came with two goalposts, each with a 'goalkeeper' fixed to a wire frame, along which he could be moved horizontally and around which he could be spun to save a shot from the opposing team. Two teams of children played against one another; they blew a small wooden (later plastic) ball along the table using wooden or cardboard tubes and tried to score a goal.

Skipping ropes

Skipping ropes could be simple pieces of rope. Some home-made skipping ropes had handles to protect the user's hands; they were made from anything available (for example, bobbins used for wool and cotton, especially in areas where there were mills). During the childhood of the children's grandparents, manufactured skipping ropes were available. They were usually made from plain smooth rope (often white or cream) with carved wooden handles. The rope was passed through the top, rounded part of the handle and fixed by means of a knot, and then the shaft of the handle was screwed into the rounded part. There were superior models with tiny ball bearings inside the handles, allowing the rope to turn more freely. By the late 1950s plastic skipping ropes with plastic handles were becoming available.

It is useful to discuss the meanings of 'old' and 'new' with the children. Point out that many things we call 'old' are 'broken' or 'outgrown'. Point out that many old things can be in perfect condition and show the children examples. Discuss how we can tell that they are old. The children might not know that certain materials, such as plastics, were not invented until about 60 years ago. Also point out differences in style between old and new toys (this is noticeable, especially in model toys such as cars and household items). Another difference is in the technology – electronic toys are fairly recent.

Old and new toys

History objectives (Unit 1)
- To describe the characteristics of old and new objects.
- To sort objects in different ways [sort toys into 'old' and 'new' sets].
- To speak about everyday objects in the past.
- To use everyday words and phrases to describe an artefact.
- To speak about how they have found out about old and new toys.
- To sequence objects in time.

Resources

- A collection of labelled modern toys and old-fashioned toys (ideally include older versions of modern toys such as cars, bikes, skates, dolls, dolls' prams, teddy bears and fluffy animals to enable direct comparisons to be made)
- Pictures of modern and old toys from retailers, websites and museums (including specialist toy museums and museums of childhood)
- Two plain boxes labelled 'old' and 'new'; they could be made to look like an old and a new toy box and labelled 'toy box'
- Cards on which are written adjectives such as 'broken', 'clean', 'dusty', 'rusty' and 'shiny'
- Scissors and glue
- Generic sheet 1 (page 18)
- Activity sheets 1–3 (pages 19–21)
- A chart for each group, on which they can glue pictures of toys

Starting points: whole class

Ask the children to choose a modern toy and name it. Then ask them to see if they can find an old toy with the same name. Discuss how they can tell which is old and which is new. Help them to ask questions that will show these differences, such as 'What is it made from?', 'Is it worn out or broken?', 'Has the colour faded?', 'Does it look old-fashioned?' They might notice signs of wear and tear on the toy. Introduce the idea that old toys might sometimes still look like new and ask them about toys they or their brothers or sisters have had for a long time and looked after well.

Show the children the cards on which are written the adjectives 'broken', 'clean', 'dusty', 'rusty' and 'shiny', and use them to describe some of the toys in the collection. Ask if they can add any adjectives.

Invite the children to talk about the old version of the toy. Draw their attention to any important details and talk about how the old toy is different from a modern one, focusing on what it looks like, the materials and the way it is made. Questions to ask include:

- Is this a new toy or an old one?
- How can we tell by looking at it?
- What colours can you see on it?
- What is it made from?
- Which parts of it are different from modern toys?
- How are these parts different?
- How is the toy like other old things? (For example, you could draw attention to old and modern styles of clothing seen on dolls; old and modern cars represented in toy cars; old and modern baby equipment used with dolls – prams, feeding bottles and so on.)

After some of the children have talked about an old and a modern toy, hold up one toy (or a picture of a toy) at a time and ask them if it belongs in the 'old' or the 'new' toy box. Invite them to take turns to place a toy in the appropriate toy box.

Give the children copies of Generic sheet 1 (page 18) and read the information with them. Ask them if they can recognise any of the toys in the pictures, and if they can see any of these toys in the classroom. Ask the children to suggest where they can find out more about old toys.

Tell the children that they are now going to work in groups cutting out pictures of toys and sorting them into 'old' and 'new'.

Ask the children to cut out a picture of an old toy and a picture of a new toy, glue them onto their group chart and write a label for each toy.

Group activities

Tell the children that they are now going to look at some pictures of toys and decide if they are old or new.

Activity sheet 1

This is for children who can recognise and copy the words 'old' and 'new' and can use simple criteria to decide whether a toy is old or new. Read the sheet with them. If they are able, they could write labels for the pictures. On the back of the sheet they have to draw another old toy and another new toy and write 'old' or 'new' below each picture.

Activity sheet 2

This is for children who can recognise and copy words they have learned about toys, as well as the high frequency words 'a' and 'an'. Read the sheet with them. They have to write simple descriptive captions and use simple criteria to decide whether a toy is old or new by its style. On the back of the sheet they have to draw and label another old toy and another new toy.

Activity sheet 3

This is for children who can recognise and write words they have learned about toys, as well as the high frequency words 'this' and 'has'. They can talk about some of the criteria they use to decide whether a toy is old or new. They have to write simple sentences. On the back of the sheet they have to draw and label another old toy and another new toy.

Plenary session

Invite the children who completed Activity sheets 1 and 2 to read out the labels or captions they wrote for each toy. How could they tell that it was old or new? Ask the class to check if they are right. The children who completed Activity sheet 3 could read out their sentences about the toys. Ask the others if they notice anything else about which they could have written. Draw out the differences between the styles of old and new toys and between the materials from which they might have been made.

Display the children's pictures and writing from the backs of the Activity sheets.

Ideas for support

To help the children identify the differences in style between the old and new car and doll, ask them questions such as: 'Which car looks like a car people might drive today?' Point to the old car. 'What is different about this car to today's cars? Is it the same?'

Ideas for extension

Invite an adult who has kept some of his or her old toys (or who has pictures of them) to come in and talk to the children. The visitor could talk about toys received as presents, memories of playing with the toys and how they had to be looked after. The visitor could talk about the differences between the toys of his or her childhood and modern toys.

Show the children examples (or pictures) of toys no longer in common use and introduce their names: for example, hobbyhorse, jack-in-the-box, top and whip.

Take photographs of the toys. The children could start a toy timeline with the photographs, starting with their own and working backwards to include parents' and grandparents' toys.

Linked ICT activities

Use *Clicker 4* or *Textease 2000* to create word-banks on screen. (See References and resources on page 89.) Enter the words that the children have used to describe the toys. You could produce different banks for different levels. Both *Clicker* and *Textease* are open-ended, allowing you to enter any number of word banks, using any words that you want to.

Ask the children to choose a toy from the 'old' or the 'new' box and place it next to the computer. Using the word banks to help them, ask the children to write about their toy. Use prompts such as 'What colour is your toy?', 'What does your toy feel like?' Print out the texts and display them under the heading 'What am I?' Ask the children to guess the toys from the descriptions.

Look at photographs of old and new toys on the toymuseum and pollocksweb websites, or on the *All About Toys* CD-Rom (see References and resources on page 89).

Old toys

Children many years ago had some toys like yours.

They had dolls.

They had dolls' prams.

They had tabletop games, like 'Blow Football'.

They had toy cars and trucks.

They had skipping ropes.

Name _____

Old or new?

Write ⬚old⬚ or ⬚new⬚ below each picture.

On the back of this sheet, draw another old toy and another new toy.
Write 'old' or 'new' below each picture.

Name _____

Old or new?

Write a label for each toy. Use the word bank to help you.

a

a

WORD BANK

a   an   doll   new   old   toy car

On the back of this sheet, draw another old toy and another new toy.
Write a caption below each picture.

Name _____

Old or new?

Write a sentence about each toy. Use the words in the boxes to help you.
You can add words of your own.

	This _____ toy car has _____ | old | | new | | wheels | | lights |
	This _____ toy car _____ _____ | old | | new | | wheels | | lights |
	This _____ doll _____ | old | | new | | long | | dress |
	This_____ doll _____ | old | | new | | long | | dress |

On the back of this sheet, draw another old toy and another new toy.
Write a label below each picture.

22

CHAPTER 3

A toy museum

Edinburgh Museum of Childhood

An example of a museum with collections of toys from the past is the Museum of Childhood in Edinburgh's Royal Mile. For details and a list of other museums, see References and resources on page 88.

Many museums have sections devoted to toys or the lives of children in the past; it is worth checking what is offered by your local museum. This chapter helps you to make the most of collections in local museums and in museums specifically devoted to children or toys (or even particular types of toy, such as teddy bears, dolls or dolls' houses). This chapter uses the Museum of Childhood in Edinburgh as an example. The following headings can be used to organise information about your local museum of toys or childhood or one of those sections in a general museum.

The founder

Joseph Patrick Murray (1908–81), a member of Edinburgh City Council, who founded the Edinburgh Museum of Childhood, was said not to like children! What made him want to start a museum of childhood was hearing, in 1955, about two dolls, once owned by Queen Victoria, that had been kept in Scotland for many years and that were going to be sent to a London museum because there was no suitable place in Scotland in which to display them.

The story of the museum

He persuaded committee members of the Lady Stairs Museum in Edinburgh to make space available to display a collection of objects connected with all aspects of the lives of children in the past. He began with his own old toys and those of friends. It was a small and rather bedraggled collection, but before long people had donated enough items to turn it into an interesting display. It grew so much that the Museum of Childhood had to move to a larger building.

This story might inspire the children (or the school) to create a permanent toy museum. This could become a valuable resource for other classes working on the topic in the future.

The Museum of Childhood in Edinburgh was the first in the world to be devoted completely to the history of childhood (although there were others devoted to toys). Joseph Murray, who was an optician, spent a great deal of time collecting items for it, researching them, labelling and cataloguing them and organising the displays. He produced a guidebook and found ways in which to advertise the museum. It began to attract many visitors.

The creation of a school or class toy museum could involve the children in collecting toys (along with information about them), finding out more about them, cataloguing them, organising the displays and writing labels for them. During a literacy lesson the children could write letters or posters asking people if they can help by donating old toys. They could also contribute to guidebooks and advertisements to tell other children, parents and friends of the school about the toy museum.

The toy collections in the Edinburgh Museum of Childhood are organised as follows:

Gallery 1: Riding toys, push and pull toys, dolls' prams, yachts and boats, money boxes; it also displays the story of the museum and items connected with babies and health.
Gallery 2: Moving toys, musical toys, optical toys, marionettes, toy vehicles, dolls' houses, toy animals (zoo, farm and circus), trains, toy theatres, toy soldiers.
Gallery 3: Dolls, soft toys, automata (mechanical toys – usually clockwork).
Gallery 4: Collecting, skills and hobbies, arts and crafts, indoor games, construction toys; it also houses artefacts connected with reading and writing, clubs and organisations, samplers and needlework.
Gallery 5: Fancy dress, in the street; it also houses items connected with the nursery and schoolroom, children and their clothes.

A toy museum

LESSON PLAN

History objectives (Unit 1)
- How museum exhibits are organised.
- To sort objects in different ways.
- To communicate what they have learned about toys.
- That museum displays can be used to find out about the past.
- To speak about how they have found out about old and new toys.

Resources

- A collection of old toys (borrowed from, or donated by, children's families and friends of the school, or from jumble sales and car boot sales) including musical, indoor, making and riding toys
- A guidebook from a museum to be visited (or the Edinburgh Museum of Childhood) and pictures of the toys on display there
- Generic sheet 1 (page 25)
- Activity sheets 1–3 (pages 26–28)

Starting points: *whole class*

Ideally, take the children to a museum with a collection of toys. Otherwise, show them pictures of such a museum, and tell them about it (for example, using the information provided about the Edinburgh Museum of Childhood). Before (or instead of) the visit, discuss the children's experiences of museums. Do they know what a museum is? Write the word 'museum' on the board, say it and ask the children to repeat it. What kinds of things have they seen in museums? Ask them if they have seen toys in museums; if so, what they remember about them.

Tell the children that they are going to look at the museum's collections of toys from the past, and ask them what they think they might see. Draw on their experiences of looking at old toys in school. During the visit, encourage the children to make pictorial lists of the toys they see and like, or show them pictures of the toys in a museum. Adult helpers on a visit could help the children to label the pictures they draw. Encourage the children to ask questions about the toys and help them to find the answers by examining the exhibits. Ask:

- Which toy would you like to play with?
- Who might have played with this toy? (Babies, children of the children's own age, younger or older.)

- Where might they have played with it? (Indoors or outdoors, in a large space, on a tabletop.)
- How might they have used it?

Adult helpers on the visit could record the children's comments about the toys (using a cassette recorder or pencil and paper). Ask the children to describe their favourite toy from the museum. What do they like about it? How would they use it, with whom and where? Discuss any similarities between these and the children's own toys.

Tell the children about the beginnings of the Edinburgh Museum of Childhood (or about the formation of another museum devoted to toys) and read Generic sheet 1 with them (page 25). Discuss other toys, especially those from the class collection, that would fit in each category. Tell the children that they are going to begin a museum of toys.

Talk about the ways in which the toys in the Edinburgh museum were grouped: for example, cars and other vehicles, dolls, teddy bears, toys for making and learning and so on. Invite the children to sort the class collection into groups which could form the basis of different displays in different rooms. Which toys belong together, and why? With the children, write labels for each collection.

Discuss the ways in which the Edinburgh museum (or another museum) gives people information about the toys in its collection. How do visitors know what the toys are, when they were made and where they came from? Point out the need for labels; help the children to label one of the toys.

Ask the children to arrange some of the toys from the class collection in a large timeline on the floor, starting with the oldest toy they can find.

Tell the children that they are now going to look at pictures of old toys (or the toys themselves) and say what they can learn about the past from the toys. To encourage learning ask questions such as:

- Which toys show us what people wore?
- Which toys show us what houses were like?
- Which toys tell us about transport?

The children can then present their findings as a talk to the class.

Group activities

Tell the children that they are now going to plan a toy museum.

Activity sheet 1
This is for children who can place toys from a limited selection in simple categories: 'musical toys', 'toys for making things', 'indoor games' and 'riding toys'. They have to draw the correct toy in each 'room'. On the back of the sheet they have to draw a toy museum of their own. (Don't let them spend too much time drawing the building.)

Activity sheet 2
This is for children who can arrange a given selection of toys into simple categories: 'musical toys', 'toys for making things', 'indoor games' and 'riding toys'. They have to draw the correct toy in each 'room'. On the back of the sheet, they have to write a sentence about each toy and draw a toy museum of their own. (Don't let them spend too much time drawing the building.)

Activity sheet 3
This is for children who can organise a collection of toys into simple categories: 'musical toys', 'toys for making things', 'indoor games' and 'riding toys'. They have to make drawings of the toys they choose and write captions showing their names and giving simple information about them: who played with the toy when they were children, and how the toy was used.

Plenary session

Invite the children to share the ways in which they have grouped the toys and to discuss which categories they could use in their own class museum. Encourage them to say whether each category is a good one, and why (and which toys they would display in it). Discuss ways in which the museum could be made attractive to visitors.

Ideas for support

For children who have difficulty in grouping the toys, begin with only two categories (for example, musical toys and toys for making things) and place a toy in each category. Talk about the toy in a way that explains why you have placed it in that category, and ask the children to find another toy like it: 'Can you find another toy for making music?', 'Can you find another toy that is used for making things?'

To help the children talk about the similarities between toys, place two toys in a category such as 'musical toys', discuss how they are used and ask the children how they are alike and if they can find another toy like them, and glue pictures of them on a timeline.

Ideas for extension

Help the children to make a guidebook of the class toy museum which explains to visitors what it contains and where they will find different types of toy. Some children could write information sheets to display with the toys.

Ask the children to choose a toy they would like to find out more about. Help them to write questions to find out what they want to know, and talk about where they can find the answers. Provide information books to help them.

Linked ICT activities

As part of your whole-class starting points, use the toymuseum, pollocksweb or hants.gov websites to show the children some of the toys they might see in a museum. (See References and resources on page 89.)

Let the children carefully handle the collection of old toys. Using a child-friendly digital camera (such as *Digital Dream* – see References and resources on page 89), let the children take a photograph of their chosen toy. Using a tape recorder, record the children talking about their chosen toys. Encourage them to rewind and listen to the tape and perhaps add to it. Collect the photographs in a class guidebook. Keep the tape recordings with the photographs for the children to refer back to.

A toy museum

These sets of toys are in the Museum of Childhood in Edinburgh.

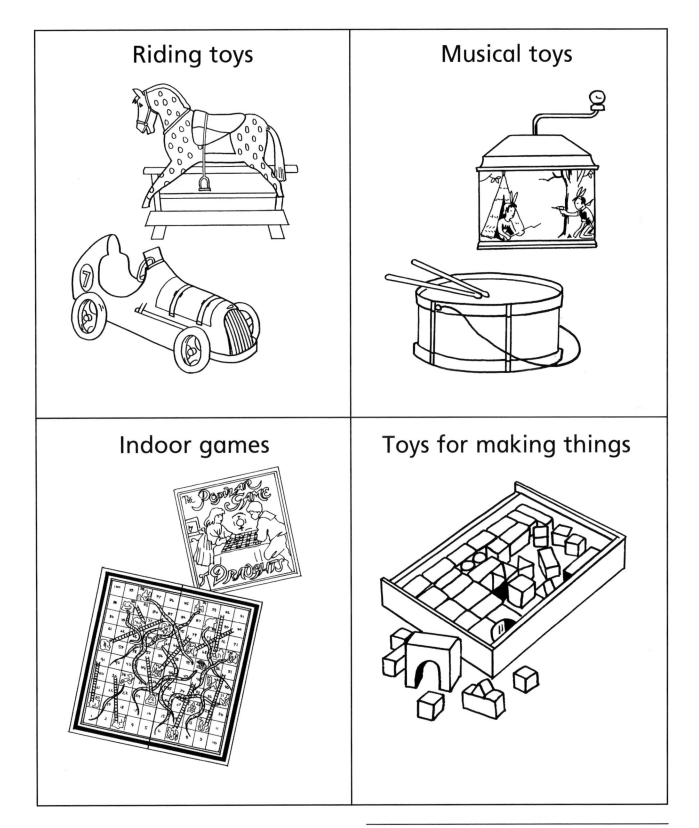

Riding toys

Musical toys

Indoor games

Toys for making things

A toy museum

Draw the toys in the correct rooms.

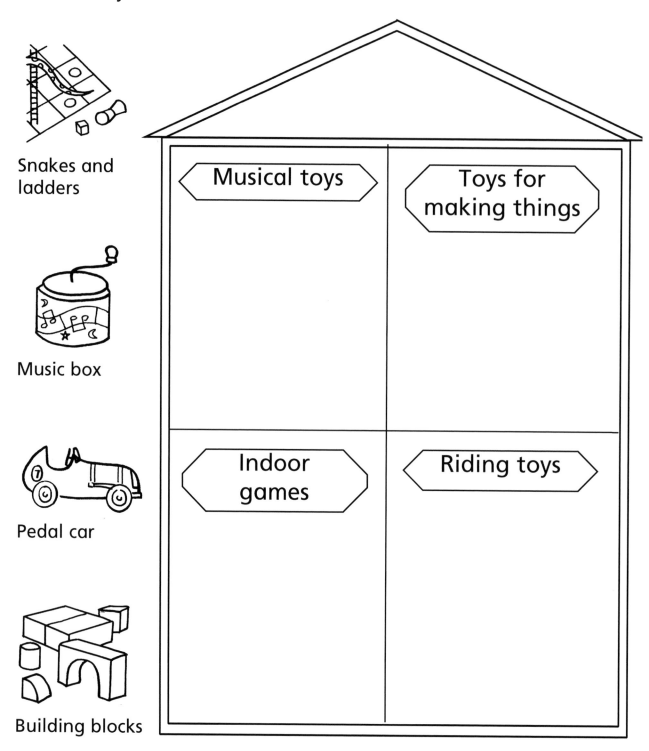

Snakes and ladders

Music box

Pedal car

Building blocks

Musical toys

Toys for making things

Indoor games

Riding toys

On the back of this sheet, draw your own toy museum with a toy in each room.

Name _____

A toy museum

Draw the toys in the correct rooms.

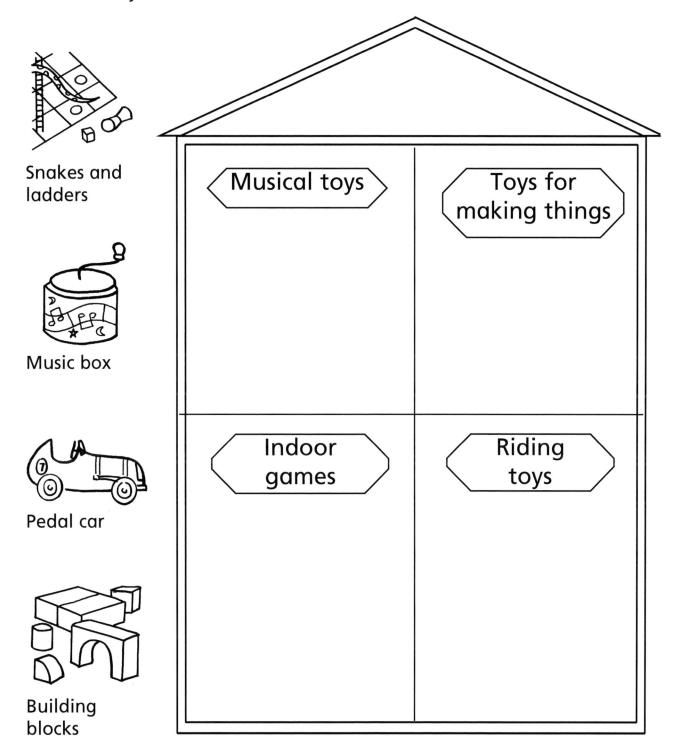

Snakes and ladders

Music box

Pedal car

Building blocks

Musical toys

Toys for making things

Indoor games

Riding toys

On the back of this sheet, write a sentence about each toy.
Then draw your own toy museum, with a toy in each room.

Name _____

A toy museum

Draw a toy in each room. Label each toy.

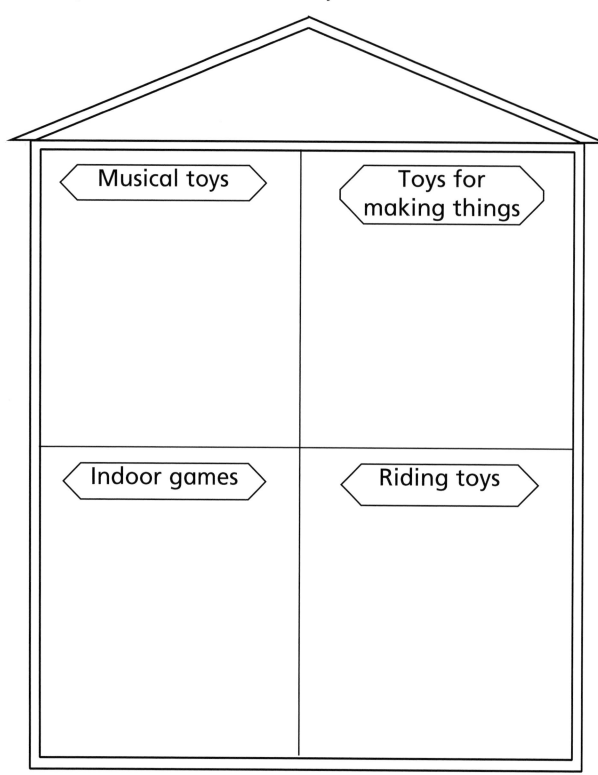

Musical toys

Toys for making things

Indoor games

Riding toys

For each toy, on the back of this sheet write about: who you think may have played with the toy as a child; how the toy was used.

Learning from pictures

CHAPTER 4

TEACHERS' NOTES

Children's skills in finding out about the past can be developed through using pictures as sources of information.

A list of pictures and books is provided in References and resources on pages 88 and 89 to help you find copies of paintings, drawings and prints that show toys from the past. Many of these sources depict children playing with the toys. Those for which discussion and activities are suggested in this chapter have been selected because they are well known and are the most easily accessible, but it is interesting to look at the others listed.

Transparencies or very large reproductions of the paintings are useful so that the children can see the toys shown in them in as much detail as possible.

Some well known and accessible pictures of toys

'Children's Games' by Pieter Breughel the Elder (1560) Kunsthistorisches Museum, Vienna. In the picture more than 230 children are playing about 90 different games, with only two adults. The children look as if they have taken over the main square of a town, the wide road and the surrounding grassland, trees and river. The toys shown in the picture include hoops, and sticks for bowling them, a hobbyhorse, tops and whips, a spinning top, marbles and bats and balls.

'Child with a Rattle' by Paul Van Somer (1611) Leeds City Art Galleries. A boy aged about two, wearing an elaborately embroidered brocade and lace pinafore over an ankle-length dress with a ruff at the neck and lace cuffs, holds a gold rattle with bells hanging from it. The rattle has a piece of ivory fixed to the end of it for use as a teether. This painting can be found in *Innocence and Experience: Images of Children in British Art from 1600 to the Present*, Manchester City Art Galleries, 1992.

'The Graham Children' by William Hogarth (1742) National Gallery, London. These are the children of Daniel Graham, apothecary to the king (George II), and therefore from a wealthy family. Poor children of that time

would not have had manufactured toys; they might have had home-made toys. The boy is playing a mechanical music box or organ of very intricate workmanship. The youngest child, on the left, is seated in a wheeled chair with a long handle which has a bird carved on it close to where her feet rest. Older children or adults could pull the chair by the handle, for the amusement of the younger child (or as a form of transport).

'John, Lord Willoughby de Broke and his Family' by Johann Zoffany (1766) Christie's. The painting shows a well-to-do family group. The mother is seated, holding a baby, with her husband standing behind her, wagging his finger at a child who is reaching for a china bowl on the table. An infant pulls a wooden horse on wheels by means of a cord.

'Cottage Scene with Children at Play' (sometimes called 'Bubbles') by John Dawson Watson (1856) Cecil Higgins Art Gallery, Bedford. In the painting a girl amuses a baby and some younger girls by blowing bubbles through a clay pipe, which she has filled from a brown earthenware jug of soapy water. A boy blows through a piece of straw to make a froth from soapy water in a white china or earthenware jug while another boy watches, fascinated, over his shoulder.

'The English Boy' by Ford Madox Brown (1860) Manchester City Art Galleries. This is a portrait of a long-haired boy wearing a straw hat and holding in one hand a wooden spinning top and in the other a wooden whip with leather thongs. This painting can be found in *Innocence and Experience: Images of Children in British Art from 1600 to the Present*, Manchester City Art Galleries, 1992.

'The Lowther Arcade' by the circle of H C Bryant (c.1870) Coutts & Co. The Lowther Arcade (now demolished) in London was a bazaar near the Strand, which contained covered walks between rows of shops stocked with toys and household articles. It was famous in

Victorian times for its toyshops. This painting can be found in several books, including *Innocence and Experience: Images of Children in British Art from 1600 to the Present*, Manchester City Art Galleries, 1992. It shows children with their parents shopping for toys. Numerous toys are included: dolls, rocking horses, pull-along horses (some large enough for a small child to ride), drums, tin whistles, bugles, brightly coloured balls, hoops, clockwork toys, model soldiers, puppets, masks and other dressing-up items, buckets and spades.

'The Lowther Arcade' by Thomas Crane and Ellen Houghton (1883) The Anthony Crane Collection, UK.

The print shows a drawing of a different view of the Lowther Arcade, with similar toys to those shown in the Bryant painting, as well as a hobby-horse, a dolls' house, yachts and bats. Generic sheet 1 (see page 33) has been based on this print.

'Bubbles' by John Everett Millais (1886) A & P Pears, London.

This famous painting, created as an advertisement for Pears soap, shows a boy dressed in velvet knickerbockers, a velvet jacket and a shirt with a frilled collar, seated on a log with a brown earthenware bowl of soapy water. He has just blown some bubbles using a long-stemmed clay pipe.

'The Day After Christmas' by Mark Symons (1931) Bury Art Gallery and Museum.

Five children aged from about three to six months to eleven or twelve years play with the toys they were given as Christmas presents. The older two girls sit at a table making an elaborate structure from a wooden construction kit. Two younger girls sprawl on the floor, one holding a doll, the other blowing a horn and holding a toy windmill. Spread over the floor are many other toys: a dolls' house, building blocks, a jack-in-the-box, model horses, dolls and paper hats. A rocking parrot on a frame stands on a chair in the background. This painting can be found in *Innocence and Experience: Images of Children in British Art from 1600 to the Present*, Manchester City Art Galleries, 1992.

Learning from pictures

LESSON PLAN

Resources

- Two or three large copies of works of art showing as many different toys as possible, or children at play in the past: paintings, prints, illustrations from children's books, drawings and photographs
- As many as possible smaller copies of works of art as described above
- Copies of the toy labels from the photocopiable word bank (pages 84–87), both with and without the illustrations
- Generic sheet 1 (page 33)
- Activity sheets 1–3 (pages 34–36)

Starting points: *whole class*

Talk about the ways in which the children have already found out about toys in the past: from other people (such as their parents/carers and grandparents and older friends of the school), museums and books.

Say that they are going to find out about toys from the past by looking at some pictures that were made a long time ago showing children and their toys.

Show a picture of children of the past with their toys, and tell the children what kind of picture it is (painting, drawing, print or photograph). Ask them what they notice about the children and how they can tell that they are from the past. Point out their clothes, hairstyles and the setting, noticing anything which might not be seen nowadays.

Talk about what the children are doing and about the toys shown in the picture. Ask the children if they can see any toys they or other children have nowadays. Encourage them to look closely at the toys and to notice how they are similar to, and different from, their modern counterparts and to describe any toys they have never seen before. Ask them what they can find out from the picture about toys they have never seen before: what they

are made from, what they look like and how they are used. Tell the children the names of the toys and explain how they were used.

Show them other pictures of children of the past with their toys and discuss them in a similar way. Questions to ask include:

- How can we tell that this picture is from the past?
- Is it from when your grandparents were children or is it from before that?
- How can we tell?
- Are the children boys or girls?
- What are the children wearing? (Note that boys up to the early twentieth century wore dresses until they were three to five years old.)
- What toys can you see?
- Are they like any of your toys?
- How are they like your toys?
- How are they different?
- What are the children doing with the toys?
- How are they playing with them?
- Are there any toys you have never seen before?

Read Generic sheet 1 (page 33) with the children, and help them to read the signs. Which of the toys in the picture have they seen in other pictures from long ago?

Give out a selection of small pictures showing children from the past and their toys. Ask the children if they can find particular types of toys: for example, a hoop, a skipping rope, a toy animal, a bat or a ball. Ask them if they can find any other kinds of toys and if they can name them. Encourage them to refer to Generic sheet 1 and the photocopiable word bank (see pages 84–87) to find the names of the toys and to spell them.

Group activities

Tell the children that they are now going to use pictures to find out about toys and games from long ago. Show the children the picture on the Activity sheets and ask them how we can tell that the children are from a long time ago (if necessary, point out their clothes and discuss how they differ from children's clothes of today).

Activity sheet 1

This is for children who can identify toys from the past and match them to their names on an illustrated list. Ask them what other toys, not on the list, they can see in the picture. Also ask them why they think some of the toys on the list are not in the picture and remind them that a long time before their grandparents were born there were no cars or planes. On the back of the sheet they have to draw and label two other toys from the picture.

Activity sheet 2

This is for children who can use their previous learning to name the toys they can see in an old picture and can use the photocopiable word bank to find the names of the toys (see pages 84–87). They have to circle the old toys in the picture and list six of them. They have to name some toys that children long before their grandparents were born could not have had, and say why.

Activity sheet 3

This is for children who are developing an understanding of the differences between toys of the past and those of today. They are beginning to distinguish between the styles of old and modern toys and are developing an awareness of the timescale of inventions such as computers, television, aircraft and spacecraft. They have to circle the toys from long ago in green and the toys that do not belong in the picture in red. They have to list the toys. On the back of the sheet they have to list some toys that were invented long ago but are still used today (boat, doll, dolls' house, skipping rope, toy horse).

Plenary session

Invite the children to talk about what they have learned from the pictures about toys from a long time before their grandparents were born. Which toys did the children in the pictures have? Which ones were similar to modern toys? Which modern toys did the children in the pictures not have? Which toys in the pictures do the children have themselves today?

Ideas for support

For children who can talk about the toys from the past which they can see in pictures, but do not know what they are called, provide cards made from the photocopiable word bank, read the words with them and ask them to match the cards to the toys in the pictures.

The children could draw a picture of a birthday present or a gift for a festival such as Christmas or Id-al-Fitr from long before their grandparents were born, and write a gift label to fix on to it. Ask them to write a caption for the picture.

Ideas for extension

Create a 'toyshop from long ago' in the classroom in which old toys can be bought and sold. The children could make labels for the toys. Alternatively, create a life-sized display entitled 'A toyshop from long ago', for which the children can paint or draw pictures of toys they see in copies of works of art or photographs from long ago. They could add their pictures to their toys timeline.

Ask the children to choose a picture to write about, and help them to write a non-chronological report about the toys in the picture for a class book about toys from the past.

Linked ICT activities

On the toypost, toymuseum, pollocksweb or hants.gov websites (see References and resources on page 89), the children can look at some old toys, with descriptions of how they worked. Discuss some of the toys with the children, asking them how they would play with the toys (spin, shake, roll, bounce). Use a tape recorder to record the children's thoughts about how they would feel if these were the only toys they had to play with. Which would be their favourite toy, and why? Invite some grandparents/great grandparents into class. Play them the recording. Ask them to comment. Did they feel they were missing out at the time, or were they happy with the toys they had?

Toyshops from long ago

This picture shows toyshops in London more than 100 years ago.
This is before your grandparents or even their grandparents were born.
It shows children from rich families choosing toys.

Name _____

Playtime long ago

What toys can you see in the picture?   ☑

🏏	Bat and ball ☐	⭕	Hoop ☐
🚬	Bubble pipe ☐	✈️	Plane ☐
🚗	Car ☐	🪢	Skipping rope ☐
🧍	Doll ☐	🚂	Train ☐

On the back of this sheet, draw and label two other toys from the picture.

Name _____

Playtime long ago

Circle the old toys in the picture. List six toys from the picture.
Use the word bank your teacher gives you to help you.

1.

2.

3.

4.

5.

6.

On the back of this sheet, name three toys the children in this picture
could not have had. Say why.

Name _____

Playtime

- Circle the old toys in green.
- List the old toys.

- Circle the new toys in red.
- List the new toys.

_____ | _____

_____ | _____

_____ | _____

_____ | _____

_____ | _____

On the back of this sheet, list some toys in the picture that were invented long ago and are still used today.

Teddy bears

TEACHERS' NOTES

Teddy bears first appeared under that name in 1903, although there had been soft toys in the form of bears (often called 'bruins') for some time.

There is a well known story about a time when President Theodore (Teddy) Roosevelt of the USA went to Mississippi, in November 1902. On the first day of the hunt the president refused to shoot a healthy 235-pound female bear that had been chased for four hours and had then fought against the hunting dogs. The hunt guide had clubbed the bear to save his dogs, and then tied it up and offered it to the president, who refused to shoot it. Instead, he directed a hunter to end its life with a knife. The bear was taken back to the Smithsonian Institute in Washington for study, where it remains today.

The incident became the subject of a cartoon by Clifford K Berryman, which appeared in the *Washington Post* on 16 November 1902. The caption to this famous cartoon 'Drawing the line in Mississippi' was a *double entendre* referring to both the hunt and a boundary dispute between Mississippi and Louisiana going on at the time.

As soon as they saw the cartoon, the New York sweets, stationery and novelty sellers Morris and Rose Michtom made a stuffed plush velvet bear and placed it for sale (labelled 'Teddy Bear') in the window of their store alongside a copy of the cartoon.

The bear proved so popular that they were hard-pressed to keep up with demand, so they formed the Ideal Toy & Novelty Company to manufacture teddy bears. Morris Michtom wrote to the president asking permission to use his name for the bear; Roosevelt is reported to have replied, 'I doubt if my name will mean much to the cub bear business, but you may use it if you wish.'

Even the early teddy bears had limbs made to swivel on rotating joints in which the limbs were joined to the body with string-fastened disks. Some had skins made from sheepskin, rather than plush velvet, with velvet pads on their paws, and were stuffed with straw. Their noses and mouths were stitched in black thread, although sometimes the noses were made from black sealing wax. Their eyes were made from black boot buttons. Many of them had 'growling' mechanisms inside their bodies. By the 1930s straw stuffing had given way to kapok and the eyes began to be made from glass, but the noses and mouths continued to be stitched in black thread. Plastic noses were introduced later.

Among the first European manufacturers were Steiff in Germany; Merrythought and Chad Valley in Britain followed. All of them still make teddy bears today.

After the Second World War, manufacturers began to make bears from synthetic fabrics such as nylon, and with fixed limbs. It was not until the late 1970s that the traditionally styled teddy bear was reintroduced, due to consumer demand.

In the 1950s, Wendy Boston Playsafe Toys introduced the 'safe eye' and made machine-washable teddy bears.

LESSON PLAN

Teddy bears

Resources

- A collection of teddy bears (the children's own and any they can bring in belonging to their parents/carers or grandparents and older friends of their families)
- Pictures of modern and old teddy bears
- Labels: 'old', 'new', 'oldest', 'newest'
- *Old Bear* by Jane Hissey (Red Fox, 1991) or *Threadbare* by Mick Inkpen (Hodder, 1990), or another picture storybook about a teddy bear made a long time ago
- Generic sheets 1–3 (pages 41–43)
- Activity sheets 1–3 (pages 44–46)

Starting points: *whole class*

Tell the children that they are going to find out about the differences between teddy bears made a long time ago and new ones, and that first they are going to hear a story about a teddy bear made a long time ago.

Read one of the stories about an old teddy bear to the children, showing them the pictures. Talk briefly about the children's responses to the story before showing them the cover of the book and asking them how we can tell that this is an old teddy bear. The children should notice if its fur has worn off in places (introduce the word 'threadbare'), whether it has been patched or repaired in any way, and whether its eyes are made from glass beads or buttons or are stitched with black thread.

Compare the old teddy bear from the story with some of the old bears in the classroom collection and notice any similarities: for example, the ways in which the arms and legs are joined to the body, the materials from which the body and paws are made (notice that Old Bear's claws are stitched with lines of black thread), the materials from which their

eyes, noses and mouths are made and the stuffing inside them (notice how it feels when squashed). When any materials are mentioned, write the words in a word bank.

Compare the old teddy bear in the story and the old teddy bears in the classroom collection with the new ones, drawing attention to the ways in which their arms and legs are joined to their body, the materials from which the body and paws are made, the materials from which their eyes, noses and mouths are made and the feel of the stuffing inside them.

Discuss the fact that 'old' doesn't necessarily have to mean worn out/threadbare. Remind the children that a new bear could soon become damaged and that some very old bears can still be in good condition.

Questions to ask include:

- Is this teddy bear old or new?
- How can we tell?
- What is its body made from?
- What are its paws made from?
- What do you notice about the colours of very old teddy bears?
- What do you notice about the colours of new teddy bears?
- What do you notice about the eyes of old teddy bears?
- What do you notice about the eyes of new teddy bears?

Invite the children to talk about their own teddy bear. Ask them if it has a name and if it was bought new for them or if it used to belong to someone else. The others can help to decide if it is a new or an old teddy bear.

Compare old and new teddy bears by sharing Generic sheets 1 and 2 (pages 41 and 42) together with teddies from the collection. Draw attention to their arms and legs (noting if they move or turn in any way); the fabric from which their bodies and paws are made; the stuffing (how soft it feels when squashed); the materials used for the eyes, nose and mouth; whether they can make a sound (or if they used to make a sound when they were new); and their colours. You could discuss how today there are new bears made to look like old-fashioned bears and that these bears are new ones.

Group activities

Share the story 'Gran's teddy bear' on Generic sheet 3 (page 43) with the children. Discuss how he is different from, or the same as, their own teddy bears. Tell them that it will help them with the writing they are going to do. Tell them that they are now going to compare an old-fashioned teddy bear with a new one.

Activity sheet 1
This is for children who, with help, can copy words from a word bank onto the appropriate labels. Read the labels with them. They know that old-fashioned teddy bears are different from new ones.

Activity sheet 2
This is for children who can write captions using words supplied in a word bank. They know about some of the features of old-fashioned teddy bears and about some of the ways in which they are made. On the back of the sheet they have to write a sentence about the new teddy bear.

Activity sheet 3
This is for children who can use sources such as word banks and texts they have read to find the spellings of words they want to write. They can recognise some of the features of old-fashioned and new teddy bears. They have to write sentences about the characteristics of the old and new teddy bears depicted.

Plenary session

Ask the children what they have learned about the differences between old and new teddy bears and discuss how they know. Reinforce the ways in which they found the information – from other people, from books and by looking at real teddies.

Help the children to arrange a set of three or four teddy bears in order, from oldest to newest (place the labels 'oldest' and 'newest' at each end of the line). Discuss how they know which is the oldest and which is the newest, reminding them that they have to think of what the bears are made from and how they are made as well as looking for wear and tear, because sometimes very old things are well looked after and new things might not be. You could photograph the timeline of teddy bears in sections, and link the photographs to make a display timeline.

Ideas for support

For children who can identify which of a pair of teddy bears is older or newer but need help in saying how they know which is which, ask them questions such as 'Is its fur wearing off?'

To help the children to work out the age order of three or four teddy bears, ask them which owner is the oldest, who is the next oldest and so on. Also remind them of modern features not seen on older teddy bears: a variety of colours, plastic noses and eyes, and so on.

Ideas for extension

Make a class teddy bear museum. The children could arrange the teddy bears in sets according to how old they are, and write captions for the sets: for example, 'Our teddy bears are new', 'Our mums' and dads' teddy bears', 'Our grandparents' teddy bears' and 'Very old people's teddy bears'. They could write descriptions of the teddy bears, noting the materials from which they are made and how they are different from the bears in other sets.

Challenge the children to find the oldest teddy bear they can. They could look in books and, with help, on websites. Tell them the story of Theodore Roosevelt and the bear. The children could retell the story of the teddy bear in words and pictures, by hand or using a word processor, and display it in the class 'teddy bear museum'.

Linked ICT activities

Use the websites teddymatters and oldbear (see References and resources on page 89) as a starting point with the children. These contain many photographs of teddy bears old and new. Talk about the pictures. Ask:

- What are the teddy bears wearing?
- How do we know whether they are old or new?

Use the program *My World for Windows* and the file called 'dressted' (see References and resources on page 89). Give the children the opportunity to explore the program, which allows them to create a picture of their own teddy bear, dragging and dropping different items of clothing onto the bear. Having completed their teddy bear, they can print out the final picture.

Using a word processing or writing program, ask the children to write their own name label for their teddy bear. Create a class display using the images of the teddy bears, which could be a teddy bears' picnic, a walk in the woods or a visit to the seaside, depending on the time of year and other topic areas that you may be covering in class. Ask the children to create the labels and captions for the display, using a writing program.

An old teddy bear

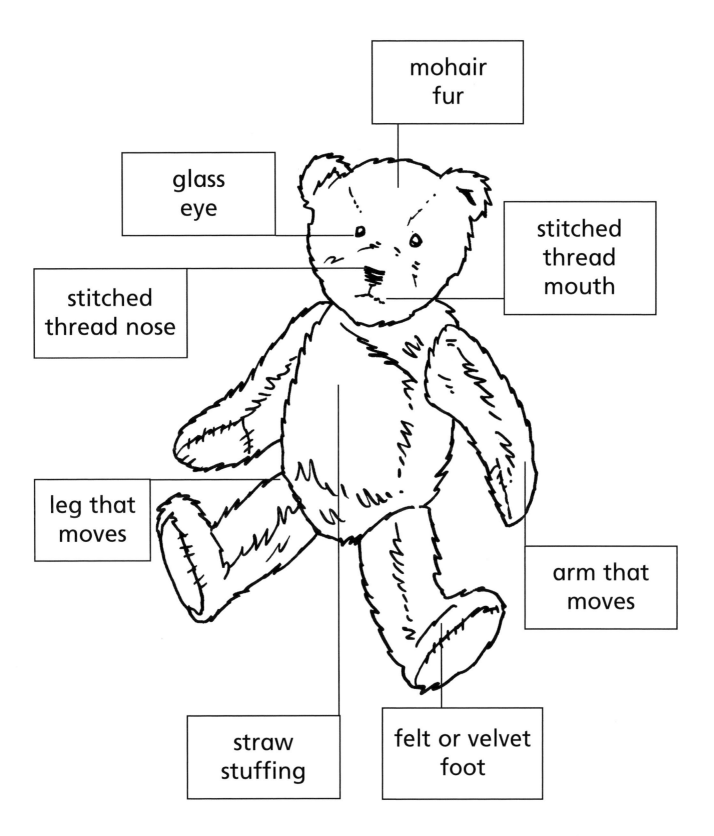

mohair
fur

glass
eye

stitched
thread
mouth

stitched
thread nose

leg that
moves

arm that
moves

straw
stuffing

felt or velvet
foot

A new teddy bear

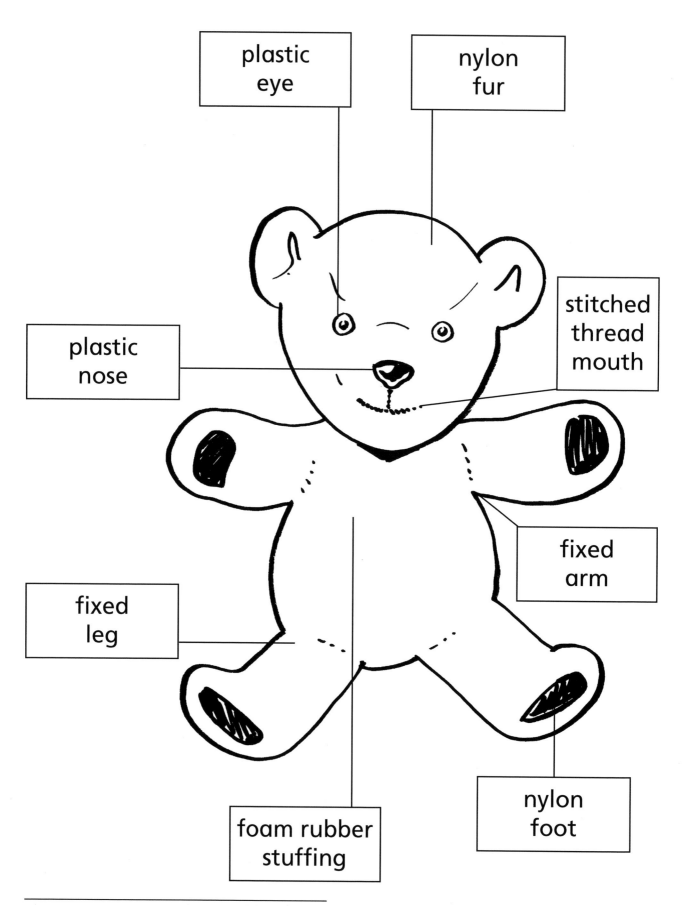

plastic
eye

nylon
fur

stitched
thread
mouth

plastic
nose

fixed
arm

fixed
leg

foam rubber
stuffing

nylon
foot

Gran's teddy bear

My grandmother bought my teddy bear for me when I was born. That was in 1939 – a long time ago.

His fur was made from a material made to look like real fur. It was golden brown and curly. His paws were made from velvet.

His body felt soft on the outside but it was quite hard inside. It was stuffed with straw.

His eyes were made from black glass beads stitched to his head. They came off and got lost.

My mum made new eyes for him. She sewed two buttons onto his face.

Gran's teddy
His name was George.

His nose and mouth were stitched in black thread.

His arms and legs were joined to his body so that they could be turned. I could just see the thick pieces of string which joined them. I used to turn his arms and legs and make him do all kinds of things. One leg came off. There was a big hole where the string had fitted in.

My grandfather sewed a leather patch onto the top of the leg and put the string back in.

The best part of my teddy was his growl. If I tipped him onto his back and then onto his front a growl came from inside him.

Name _____

Old and new bears

Complete the labels. Use the word bank to help you.

glass
_____

moving
_____

thread
_____

felt
_____

an old bear

plastic
_____

fixed
_____

plastic
_____

nylon
_____

a new bear

WORD BANK			
foot	arm	eye	nose

Name _____

Old and new bears

Write labels for the old teddy bear. Use the word bank and Generic sheet 1 to help you.

The nose is made from black

_____

The arms are fixed on with

_____

The body is stuffed with

_____

an old bear

The eyes are made from

_____

The paws are made from

_____

WORD BANK

glass   straw   string   thread   velvet

On the back of this sheet, write a sentence about the new teddy bear. Use Generic sheet 2 to help you.

a new bear

Name _____

Old and new bears

Write sentences to say what the old-fashioned teddy bear is made from. Use Generic sheet 1 to help you.

an
old-fashioned
teddy bear

1. The eyes are made from _____

2. The nose is made from _____

3. The body is made from _____

4. The body is stuffed with _____

5. The feet are made from _____

Now, on the back of the sheet, write two sentences about the new teddy bear. Use Generic sheet 2 to help you.

a new teddy bear

Models

TEACHERS' NOTES

Through studying toys modelled on real-life objects, children can learn a great deal about life in the past as well as about the toys themselves.

To prepare for comparisons between the styles of toys from the past modelled on real-life artefacts, it is useful to begin by comparing present-day toys with the real-life counterparts they represent: for example, buildings, vehicles, household equipment and clothes.

Also notice what games and models are available: for example, nowadays there are model microwave ovens and computer games based on television programmes, neither of which was available in the 1950s.

Modern 'model' toys can be compared with earlier ones, particularly vehicles and household equipment from when the children's grandparents were young.

Model washing machines, vacuum cleaners and cookers were available in the 1950s, but they looked different from the toys of today. For example, a typical washing machine from that time (such as the Hoover toy washing machine) had to be loaded from the top; the tub had to be filled via a tube attached to a tap; a large agitator rotated vertically, changing direction at intervals to move the washing around; the washing then had to be lifted out onto a drainer (which unfolded from one side of the washing machine) and then passed through a mangle (attached to the top of the washing machine). The tub had to be emptied through a tube hooked over the side of the sink.

One of the main differences between models from about 1930 to 1960 and those of today is the materials from which they are made. The better quality toy kitchen equipment and vehicles of the 1930s and even 1960s tended to be made from metal, because the plastics available at the time were brittle (see Chapter 8, Materials), whereas nowadays more robust plastics can be used and modern technology provides more sophisticated ways of colouring and joining plastics.

Dolls' houses and sets of model household equipment are particularly useful for helping the children to learn about everyday life in the past as well as about the ways in which children in times past amused themselves. The children can learn about the different styles of furniture and household equipment, and about the different items people had in the past but rarely use nowadays, if at all: carpet sweepers, hot-water bottles, washboards, and kettles for heating on the hob.

Through studying dolls' houses, the children can learn about homes from a long time before their grandparents were born, as well as homes from the childhood of their grandparents. It is important to help them to distinguish between the dolls' houses from these different ages in the past; an important difference between Victorian homes and the homes of their grandparents' childhood is that the latter had electricity, which affected many items of household equipment.

Model toys from the past reflect inventions such as the telephone, radio and television.

Models

History objectives (Unit 1)

- To speak about everyday objects in the past.
- How to find out about aspects of the past.
- That oral sources can be used to find out about the past.
- To use everyday words and phrases to describe an artefact.

Resources

- A collection of modern toys modelled on real-life artefacts: dolls' houses, replicas of other buildings, domestic and workplace equipment, vehicles, aeroplanes, spacecraft and boats, dolls' clothes and dressing-up outfits
- A collection of toys from the past modelled on real-life artefacts: telephones, furniture, cookers, washing machines, carpet sweepers, vacuum cleaners and vehicles
- Pictures of toys from each of the above categories (from toy museums, books, retail brochures, mail order catalogues and websites)
- Generic sheet 1 (page 51)
- Activity sheets 1–3 (pages 52–54)

Starting points: *whole class*

Tell the children that they are going to look at toys modelled on real-life things. Ask them if any of their toys are meant to be like real-life things.

Invite the children to choose a toy from the collection of modern toys and to say what it is, what makes it realistic, and if they can think of anything that would make it more so. Ask the class if they think this toy is old or new, and how they can tell. Do they think their grandparents had toys of that kind?

Questions to ask include:

- Is this toy old or new?
- How can we tell by looking at it?
- What real-life thing is it like?
- Is it the same as the real-life thing?
- What differences are there between the toy and the real thing?
- Is it made from the same material as the real thing?
- Does it work or do you have to pretend?
- How could you use it?
- When would you play with it?

Discuss everyday things invented since the children's grandparents were young, and write on the board the children's ideas (do not correct any of their misconceptions, but ask them how they can find out if they are right). Explain that since the children's grandparents were young many new things, such as microwave ovens and mobile phones, have been invented. Can they think of anything else? Examples of inventions to be checked by asking their grandparents or other older people known to your school include batteries, cars, electricity, radio, telephones (and mobile phones), television and vacuum cleaners. Explain that this would affect the types of model toys made.

Help the children to write a list of questions to ask their grandparents about their model toys and about their real-life counterparts.

Show the children the collection of older model toys and ask them if any of them are models of the same kinds of things as modern toys (for example, toy telephones, furniture, household equipment such as cookers, washing machines and vacuum cleaners or carpet sweepers), and invite them to compare the old and new versions of each item.

Tell the children that they are going to draw a picture of an old toy modelled on something real. Encourage them to talk about what they notice when they look at the toy and handle it, how it works, any important parts it has and what it is made from. The children should write a caption for their picture and label the important parts of it. Ask them to talk and write about what the toy was like to play with and how well it worked.

Tell the children that they are now going to look at a picture of an old dolls' house that is even older than the ones their grandparents might have had. Give them copies of Generic sheet 1 (page 51) and read the labels with them. Ask them which things in the dolls' house are like things they have in their own houses, and which things are different. They should notice familiar items such as beds, chairs, the table and the kitchen utensils. Ask them if they are the same as their own beds, chairs, tables, and so on. How are they different?

Ask the children if they see anything in the dolls' house that they do not see in their own houses or in other modern houses: for example, the coal scuttle, the cooking range, the chamber pot, the washstands with jugs and bowls. Emphasise that this model house is like the houses people had before most of their grandparents were born.

Group activities

Tell the children that they are now going to look at some objects in the old dolls' house and say whether those objects are used in homes today.

Activity sheet 1

This is for children who can recognise and copy the high frequency words 'yes' and 'no' and can use them to answer questions about artefacts from the past. Read the instructions with the children and ask them to look at the pictures and say what they are. Do they remember the name of the things from the old dolls' house? Read the labels with them and ask them to find the objects on the picture of the old dolls' house. Ensure that they can recognise the high frequency words 'yes' and 'no'. Model how to complete the Activity sheet by asking the children what the first picture is and whether or not they have one in their house. The answer will probably be 'yes' (albeit of a different style). Ask the children to write 'yes' and to continue in the same way for the other pictures. On the back of the sheet they have to draw and label another artefact from the old dolls' house, and say whether they have it in their house.

Activity sheet 2

This is for children who can copy simple drawings of artefacts and their labels and decide whether the artefacts belong to a dolls' house of the present day or the past. Read the instructions with the children and ask them what the pictures are. Ask them to read the labels and to say whether the objects belong to a new dolls' house or to the old dolls' house. Model how to complete the Activity sheet by asking them in which house they will draw the first object. Ask them to draw it there, copy the label and continue in the same way until they have

drawn all the objects in the correct houses. On the back of the sheet they have to draw another artefact from the new and the old dolls' houses.

Activity sheet 3

This is for children who can talk about the differences between artefacts in an old dolls' house and those in their own homes and say what we have instead. Remind them that dolls' houses are models of real ones. Ask them what the items depicted from the old dolls' house were for and if they have them in their own houses; if not, what do they have instead? They should draw and label these items. Encourage them to use topic lists in dictionaries, or provide a word bank. On the back of the sheet, they have to draw another object from the old dolls' house and the modern equivalent.

Plenary session

Invite the children who completed Activity sheet 1 to talk about the objects depicted on the sheet and to say whether or not they have them in their homes. Do the others agree, or would they give different answers? Let them explain their responses. Some of the children who completed Activity sheet 2 could show the class their completed pictures and talk about something else that might be found in each house. Ask the children who completed Activity sheet 3 to talk about the purpose of one of the items on the sheet and to say what people use instead nowadays.

Ideas for support

For children who need help in deciding on the purposes of some of the unfamiliar household artefacts, talk about where in the dolls' house on Generic sheet 1 the objects are found, and why they might be there. Talk about everyday activities in the children's homes: what can they see in the dolls' house that might be used for those activities?

Ideas for extension

The children could help to make and furnish model houses from the present day and the past (from before their grandparents were born). Provide books showing the interiors of real homes and encourage them to find or bring in items to represent them. Victorian dolls' house furniture could also be bought (from toy and museum shops) and used in both this project and in work on homes of the past.

Linked ICT activities

There are many new toys available from high street shops such as the Early Learning Centre, that represent modern household artefacts such as washing machines and CD players. In many instances these also need technology to run them (they may be operated by microchips). Give the children the opportunity to see and use some of these modern toys and explore the different ways that they work, comparing them with the toys played with by their grandparents.

Use photographs and websites for images of old and new dolls' houses, such as dollshouseshop and honeytoys (see References and resources on page 89). With the images, talk to the children about the size of the houses, the number of windows and rooms in the houses, the shapes of the windows, the number of chimneys, and so on.

Use a drawing program such as *Dazzle*, which uses shapes – squares, circles and so on (see References and resources on page 89). Let the children explore using these drawing tools to create a picture of their own dolls' house. Look back at the images on the websites (above) to remind them of the size and number of windows, the shape of the roof and so on.

An old dolls' house

This model house is from a very long time ago.

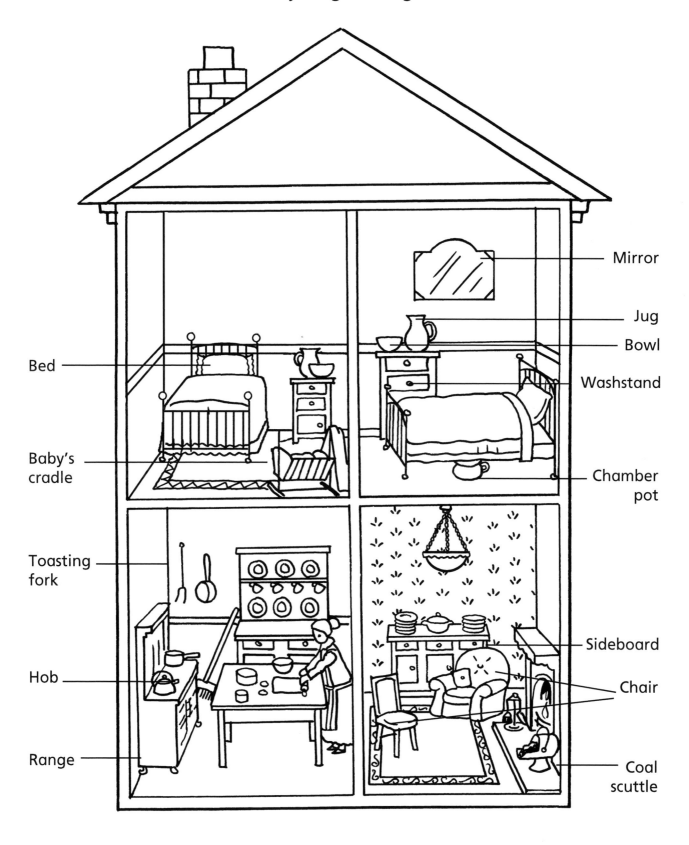

Mirror

Jug

Bowl

Washstand

Bed

Baby's cradle

Chamber pot

Toasting fork

Sideboard

Hob

Chair

Range

Coal scuttle

Name _____

The old dolls' house

Do you have these in your house?

Write [yes] or [no] .

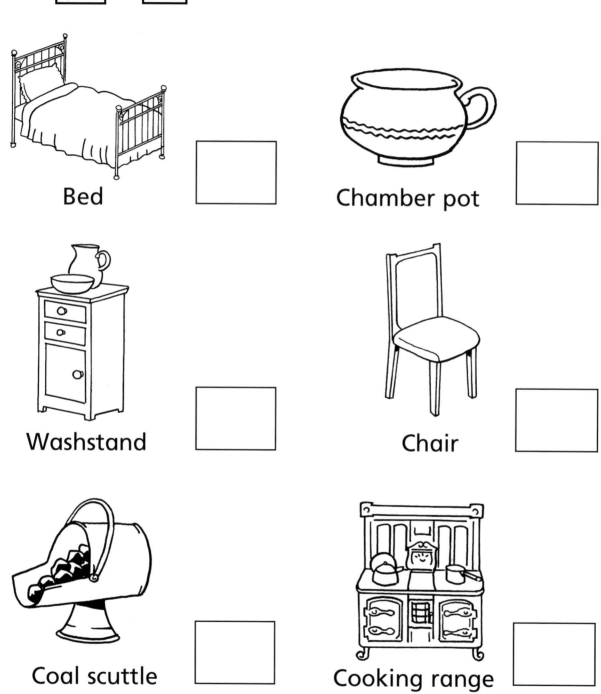

Bed ☐

Chamber pot ☐

Washstand ☐

Chair ☐

Coal scuttle ☐

Cooking range ☐

On the back of this sheet, draw and label something else from the old dolls' house.

Do you have it in your house? Write [yes] or [no] .

The old dolls' house

Which things are from an old dolls' house? Which things would be found in a new dolls' house? Draw them in the houses and label them.

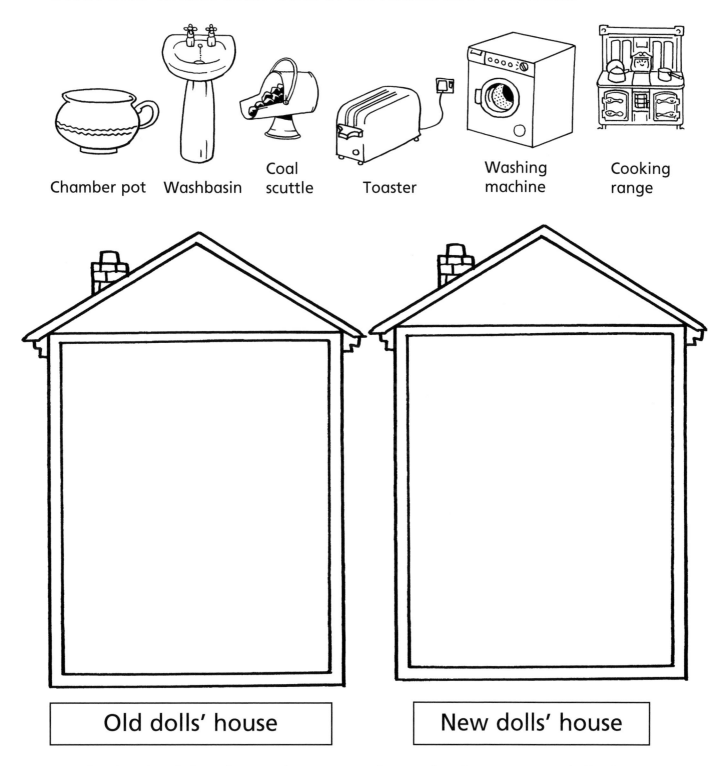

Chamber pot   Washbasin   Coal scuttle   Toaster   Washing machine   Cooking range

Old dolls' house

New dolls' house

On the back of this sheet, draw something else from a new dolls' house. Then draw something else from an old dolls' house.

Name _____

The old dolls' house

These things are from the old dolls' house.
What do you have instead in your house?

From the old dolls' house	What we have instead
A kitchen range	
A chamber pot	
A washstand	
A toasting fork	

On the back of this sheet, draw something else from an old dolls' house.
Draw what you have instead in your house.

Musical toys

CHAPTER 7

TEACHERS' NOTES

Musical toys (which include any toys designed to produce sounds) can be categorised according to the way in which the sound is produced: mechanical, shaking, tapping, beating or banging, plucking, blowing, and electronic. Some may have been seen in earlier chapters, particularly Chapter 4, Learning from pictures. (See References and resources on pages 88 and 89 for sources of the pictures mentioned below.)

Shaking

Babies' rattles have been made from various materials including wood, clay, tin plate (and, for people who could afford it, gold and silver), celluloid and, after the Second World War, plastic. An early example of a baby's rattle can be seen in the painting 'Child with a Rattle' by Paul Van Somer, painted in 1611 (Leeds City Art Galleries).

Maracas became popular as toys in the UK when large numbers of people began to take holidays abroad, particularly in Spain, during the 1960s.

Tapping, beating or banging

Children can tap or beat almost anything to make a sound, including home-made musical toys such as saucepans, tins, plant pots suspended from strings, glass bottles of water, metal bars and pieces of pipe. During the nineteenth century, when mass production became possible, toy drums made from tin plate became popular and remained so until the 1960s. Toy drums can be seen in paintings such as 'The Lowther Arcade' by the circle of H C Bryant in about 1870 and the print of the same title by Thomas Crane and Ellen Houghton from 1883. Drums were regarded as toys for boys and often used in 'pretend play' when they played at soldiers. Toy xylophones, dulcimers and pianos (including replicas of grand pianos) of different sizes can be found. They were commonly made from wood until the early twentieth century, and later from metals and plastic.

Plucking

Toy violins and guitars have been made from wood, tin plate and plastic, with strings made from animal intestine, rubber, nylon and plastic.

Blowing

Horns and bugles can be seen in paintings such as 'The Day After Christmas' by Mark Symons in 1931, 'The Lowther Arcade' by the circle of H C Bryant in about 1870 and the print of the same title by Thomas Crane and Ellen Houghton from 1883. Like many other toys, they were made from wood, tinplate and, later, plastic. Also popular (and cheap) early in the twentieth century were 'penny whistles' made from tin plate.

Mechanical

Mechanical toys of all kinds were popular in the eighteenth century when there was great public interest in science and technology and when miniature clockwork mechanisms were developed, as shown in 'The Graham Children' by William Hogarth in 1742 (National Gallery, London), in which a boy plays with a mechanical music box.

Some mechanical music boxes incorporated a dancing figure, such as a ballerina or clown, which moved while the tune played. One way to produce a sound was by means of a rotating drum (turned by hand) with spikes protruding from it which caught springy metal strips and plucked them.

Sometimes the mechanism was a bellows, which forced air through pipes or holes to produce sounds. The bellows could be operated by squeezing the toy or by tipping it upside down and then setting it upright: such as 'animal call' toys, which made, for example, the sound of a cow lowing.

Toy gramophones were produced to replicate real ones, using a stylus (needle) which followed the groove cut in the record.

These gramophones were operated in the same way as real ones: the clockwork motor was wound up using the handle. The turntable was restrained by means of a lever, which could be released once the record had been placed on the turntable and the stylus placed at the outside edge of the record.

The early record players were made from wood and metal, but one that worked in the same way was made from heavy-duty plastic from the 1970s by Fisher-Price and, like many earlier models, was powered by a clockwork motor.

Toy gramophone

In a gramophone the speaker consisted of either the enlarged part of the hollow metal arm to which the stylus was attached and which had holes bored into it, or a horn resembling a megaphone which was attached to the arm. The early toy gramophones had speakers of this type but toy record players (albeit operated by clockwork) such as the one made by Fisher-Price, had a speaker in the side of the base, like real record players.

Fisher-Price record player

The main difference between a real gramophone and a real record player is that gramophones were powered by a type of clockwork motor and the name 'record player' was given to the first electric gramophones.

Electronic

Atari were the first manufacturers to market electronic toys, in the 1970s. They produced battery-powered musical toys such as 'Simon' and 'Super Simon', which played tunes at random for children to copy and repeat. The musical game could be played at different levels, with the higher levels having a larger number of musical sounds to copy. Nowadays, there are several computer programs on the market with which children can copy sounds and put together sequences to make their own tunes.

Musical toys

LESSON PLAN

History objectives (Unit 1)

- To use everyday words and phrases to describe an artefacts
- To describe the characteristics of old objects.
- To speak about how they have found out about old and new toys.

Resources

- A collection of old and modern musical toys (including toys the children have brought in): 'bird call' toys and toys producing other animal calls, bugles, drums, electronic music makers, guitars, horns, music boxes, record players, records, gramophones and whistles
- Ideally, toys similar to those on the activity sheets, particularly those that make sounds when tipped up or when a string is pulled or a handle turned
- A CD player and discs and an old record player and vinyl records
- Magnifying glass
- Pictures of old and modern musical toys
- Generic sheet 1 (page 59)
- Activity sheets 1–3 (pages 60–62)

Starting points: *whole class*

Tell the children that they are going to look at toys designed to make musical sounds. Invite them to talk about their own musical toys, naming them and explaining how they work.

Invite them to choose an old musical toy they like. Do they know what it is called? Questions to ask include:

- Is this toy old or modern?
- How can we tell by looking at it?
- Is it like a real-life musical instrument?
- Which instrument?

Encourage the children to ask some questions of their own about the instrument by asking: 'What else would you like to know about it?' You could start them off by asking some of the following yourself:

- How old is it?
- What is it made from?

- Is it the same as a real musical instrument?
- What differences are there between the toy and the real instrument? (For example, size, material, sound.)
- Is it made from the same material as the real thing?
- What do you have to do to make the sound/ how does it work?

The children might not have seen a record player or its predecessor (a gramophone). Talk about the music their families listen to. What do they do when they want to listen to some music? Discuss the use of compact discs and CD players. Show them some vinyl records and explain how they were used; show them the groove in which the stylus (needle) ran to make the sound, and point out on a record player where the sound was heard (the speaker). Let them look at the speaker through a magnifying glass. Show the children where the batteries are fitted into a CD player and ask what happens if there are no batteries. Tell them that the old record player does not have batteries and ask if they know what makes it work.

Show the children a toy record player (for example the Fisher-Price record player from the 1980s, or a picture of it) and help them to explain how it works (by clockwork). Also show them an older toy gramophone (or a picture of one) and explain that a long time ago real record players, as well as toy ones, were powered by a clockwork motor and had to be wound up using a handle. Introduce vocabulary for talking about gramophones: handle, needle, record, speaker, turntable and lever.

Show the children an old musical toy and invite them to try it out and say how it works. Help them to express these explanations in the form of instructions: for example, 'Turn the handle'; 'Tap the drum with a stick'. Encourage them to ask some questions about it, as before.

With the children, read Generic sheet 1 (page 59). Tell them that it asks some questions about the old gramophone. Go through the questions together. (If appropriate, remind them how a question has a question mark at the end. Discuss how questions often begin with the words: 'what', 'how', 'who' and 'why'.) Can they answer any of the questions? How might they be able to find out the answers to the questions they do not know? Share the possibilities.

Group activities

Tell the children that they are now going to write their own questions about some old music boxes. Share their experiences of music boxes. Discuss how they work and what they are made from. Look at the music boxes in the collection and ask questions about them.

Activity sheet 1
This is for children who are beginning to understand how to ask relevant questions. They can talk about an old musical instrument and express their ideas about how it might work. They have to complete the sentences. On the back of the sheet, they have to write a question of their own (provide support if necessary).

Activity sheet 2
This sheet is for children who know how to ask relevant questions. They have handled musical toys and are developing an understanding of how they work. They have to label the music boxes and write two questions of their own. On the back of the sheet, they have to write questions for another music box (from the collection you have provided).

Activity sheet 3
This is for children who understand how to ask relevant questions and are confident enough to find out some answers. They have to label the music boxes, write some questions and write the answers to two of their questions.

Plenary session

Invite the children who completed Activity sheets 1 and 2 to read their completed questions. The others can listen and say if they think the questions are correct. Ask the children who completed Activity sheet 3 to read their questions aloud. Can the

others try to answer them? Discuss what the children have learned about the working of old musical toys and summarise the different ways in which the toys produce sounds: shaking, tapping (or banging or beating), plucking, blowing, by clockwork or by battery. Ask them if they can think of any other ways in which to make sounds (for example, by using their voices or scraping something).

Discuss the variety of different questions asked and remind the children of ways they could find out the answers.

Ideas for support

If children need help in writing questions, remind them how questions can begin with 'what', 'how', 'why' and 'who'. Work as a group to think up questions for each question word together.

Ideas for extension

The class collection of musical toys could be grouped in three sets ('very old', 'old' and 'new'), and then the children could arrange a set of three musical toys on a timeline labelled 'oldest' and 'newest'. They could record the timeline pictorially and then label the toys.

Ask the children to find information to help them to arrange a class timeline by asking people of different ages what musical toys they had. They could arrange pictures of the people in order from youngest to oldest and then match the toys to them.

Linked ICT activities

Show the children that you can put a music CD-Rom into a computer and the music will play just as it does in a CD player. This introduces them to the different uses of a computer.

Use the *Musical Leaps and Bounds* or *Beetles* minibeasts software (see References and resources on page 89) to introduce the children to the concept of using a computer to explore the different sounds made by different instruments.

An old gramophone

Some questions to ask about the old gramophone.

1. How old is it?

2. What does it do?

3. How do you make it work?

4. What is the handle for?

5. What is it made from?

6. Who could have owned it?

Musical toys

Complete the sentences about these music boxes.

What

_____is it?

How

_____does it work?

On the back of this sheet, write your own question about the music boxes.

Musical toys

Label the music boxes. Then read the questions.
Write a question of your own for each music box.
Use the word bank to help you.

What is it? _____

How old is it? _____

_____

_____

What is it? _____

How does it work? _____

_____

_____

WORD BANK
handle   you   string   made   from

On the back of this sheet, write questions for another music box.

Musical toys

Write labels for the music boxes.

Write some questions about them.

_____   _____

_____   _____

_____   _____

_____   _____

_____   _____

Find out the answers to two of your questions.
Write the answers here.

_____

_____

_____

_____

_____

Materials

CHAPTER 8

TEACHERS' NOTES

Plastics

The main material used for modern toys is plastic. Even the 'hair' of teddy bears and the fabrics of many soft toys can be made from plastics. Plastics are derived from petrochemicals (oil and natural gas). In a similar way to metals, they can be made into sheets, pressed into casts, joined by heat welding, poured into moulds (made from sand, clay, metal or ceramic material) and pulled into strands. They are lighter than metals, but not as strong. Plastics can be coloured while in their molten state. Rigid plastics can be machine-finished by conventional processes such as drilling, sawing, turning on a lathe and sanding. They can also be stamped from sheets using a die.

Modern plastics are rigid and strong enough for load-bearing toys, such as pedal cars, small seesaws and slides, which in the past were made from wood and metal.

The two main categories into which plastics can be divided are thermoplastic and thermosetting.

Thermoplastics can be softened or melted by heat and hardened by cooling any number of times. Articles made from thermoplastics need to be protected from heat (even from the sun).

In **thermosetting** plastics, there is a chemical reaction during the heating and softening or melting process, and after they have solidified they do not soften on further heating – they burn.

Early plastic toys, although much cheaper than metal ones, were of poorer quality. The plastic was brittle and easily broken. Designs, patterns or pictures, which were applied using paint or transfers, could be easily scraped off.

Metals

Larger modern toys, especially bicycles, scooters and larger swings, slides and seesaws tend to be made from metal, for strength.

Before plastic was available, metal was the material for making quality toy cars and trains. Steel could be die-cast to make virtually indestructible models.

Steel can be made into thin sheets, which can then be cut and beaten into the required shapes. It can be coated with tin to form tin plate. The tin coating protects the steel from rust – unless it is scratched or dented. Also made of metal were toys such as gramophones, buckets and spades for use at the seaside, music boxes, musical instruments, jack-in-the-boxes and dolls' prams.

Toy soldiers and 'cowboys and Indians' were made from lead, because it is easily poured into moulds and, when set, painted. Its use declined because of health and safety fears of lead poisoning. Lead is a soft metal, so the heads and any protruding parts of the models were easily broken off and the paint sometimes flaked off.

Rubber

Rubber was used for toys such as seaside buckets and dolls, but its use declined with the advent of plastic. Although it overcame the problems of rust and fragility, it perished after a time, becoming dry and flaky.

Ceramics

Ceramics are strong, stiff, clay-based materials that are very brittle. Skills from the pottery industry were used to make very realistic dolls' faces before plastics were available. Ceramic toys are obviously fragile, so old toys in this category are not always easy to find: examples are dolls' tea sets and some model (as opposed to toy) dolls.

Wood

Wooden toys have been made since early times. Before plastic was available, wood was one of the main materials used for models such as animals, boats, cars, dolls, dolls' houses and dolls' furniture, 'Noah's Arks', skipping rope handles, soldiers, spades for use at the seaside, tops and trains. Wooden toys are still made today and tend to be expensive because they are seen as speciality toys.

Toy power

Toys that move or produce light or sound need an energy source. That source may be human, battery, clockwork, moving water or mains electricity. Old toys (those which people older than the children's grandparents had when they were young) were mainly powered by human energy or clockwork.

For example, toy cars had to be pushed or wound up. Although batteries were available in the 1950s they were not used in many toys (apart from torches with green and red filters) until the 1960s. Popular mains electrical toys from the 1950s and 1960s include train sets and racing car sets, which used transformers to reduce the voltage to a safe level.

Toy	Power source	Toy	Power source
Swing	Human	Rally race track	Electricity
Scooter	Human	Computer game	Electricity
Rollerblades	Human	Remote-control all-terrain vehicle	Battery
Water wheel	Water	Digital percussion set	Battery
Music box	Clockwork	Sing-along music centre	Battery
Electric train set	Electricity	Robotic dog	Battery

Materials

History objectives (Unit 1)
- To describe the characteristics of old and new objects.
- To identify similarities and differences between old toys and new toys.
- To use everyday words and phrases to describe an artefact.
- To speak about how they have found out about old and new toys.

Resources

- A collection of modern toys made from different materials: ceramics, cloth, metal, plastic, wood; including some moving toys
- A collection of older toys made from different materials: cloth, metal, wood, rubber; including some moving toys
- Labelled collections of materials: ceramics, cloth, metal, plastic, rubber and wood
- Cards on which are written 'ceramics', 'cloth', 'metal', 'plastic', 'rubber' and 'wood'
- Retail toy brochures
- Generic sheet 1 (page 67)
- Activity sheets 1–3 (pages 68–70)

Starting points: *whole class*

Arrange the toys in two groups (modern toys and toys from the past), but do not label them as such.

Invite the children to come out and choose a toy from the modern set (but do not mention that these are modern toys). Ask them to notice what the toy is made from, the way it is made and how it works. Ask them if they think it is a modern toy or a toy from the past, and how they can tell. Encourage them to ask questions that will help them to find out more about the toy.

Next, repeat this with the set of toys from the past. Mention materials that were not available a long time ago and materials that were, and how they were different. What differences do the children notice?

Questions to ask include:

- What is the toy mainly made of?
- Is that a good material for it?
- Why is it a good material?

- What other materials are used for parts of the toy?
- What other materials could have been used?
- Why do you think they were not used?
- Would they have been better, and why?
- Is it a new toy or an old one?
- How can we tell?
- (where appropriate) How does it work?

Point out individual features of the toys and ask the children to name them: for example, battery, button, fur, handle, microphone, speaker, switch and wheel. Discuss the purpose of these features: for example, to make something happen, to make the toy look like a real-life item such as a tool or piece of furniture, or to look or feel good.

Give the children copies of Generic sheet 1 (page 67) and read the names of the toys and the labels indicating the materials used for the main parts of them. Ask if they are old or new, and how we can tell. Talk about other toys made from the same materials. Provide retail toy brochures for the children to cut out. Ask them to find toys that are in some way like those on the sheet. How are they alike? How are they different?

Tell the children that they are going to sort sets of modern toys according to what they are made of. Give them cards showing the name of each material, read the labels with them and ask them to put the toys next to the correct label.

Give the children another set of labels, showing the same materials, and ask them to sort the toys from the past in the same way. What similarities and differences do they notice between the two sets of toys?

Group activities

Tell the children that they are now going to choose a toy to draw, and write a caption for their picture (revise 'caption' if necessary). The Activity sheets can be used with modern toys or toys from the past.

Activity sheet 1

This is for children who need help in writing answers to questions they can answer orally. They have to choose a toy from the collection in the classroom (or their own toy). Encourage them to look at the name card beside the toy to help them to write the caption and to look at the labelled collection of materials to help them to answer the question about what it is made from.

Activity sheet 2

This is for children who can talk about their observations and are learning to express them as sentences. They have to draw and label a toy, write what the toy is made from and what colours they can see on it. On the back of the sheet, they have to draw three toys that could be made from metal.

Activity sheet 3

This is for children who can express their observations as simple sentences. They have to choose a toy that can move, then draw and label its parts and the materials it is made from. Then they have to write about why these are good materials. (Remind them of the whole-class discussion earlier.)

Plenary session

Invite the children who completed Activity sheet 1 to show their picture, read out the caption they wrote and say which boxes they have ticked on the sheet to answer each question. Ask the children to give a sentence about the material from which the toy is made and the colours they can see on it. Some of the children who completed Activity sheet 2 could read out their completed sentences. Ask the class which materials are used for making most toys, and from what materials toys might have been made before plastics were invented. Ask the children who completed Activity sheet 3 to share some of the sentences they wrote about their moving toys. The rest of the class can listen and then name some of the things that make the toys move.

Ask the children to group the collection of old toys by the materials they are made from.

Ideas for support

For children who need help in identifying materials and learning the names for them, point to the labelled collections of materials and ask them from which material their toy is made. Say the name of the material and ask the child to repeat it.

On Activity sheets 1 and 2, the colours named on the pages could be underlined using the appropriate colour.

Ideas for extension

Explore the mechanisms of moving toys, comparing modern toys and toys from the past. The children could bring in moving toys and explain how they work. If possible, provide modern toys for the children to take apart so that they can investigate the mechanisms. They could make labelled drawings of toys they have taken apart. Point out that they should not take their own toys apart in case they damage them or there is something inside on which they could hurt themselves.

Provide a collection of moving toys from the past and explore how they work. If possible take some of them apart so that the children can investigate the mechanisms. They could make labelled drawings of the mechanisms of toys from the past and compare them with those they made of modern toys.

Help the children to make moving toys from cardboard which include simple devices such as levers, sliding mechanisms and springs: examples include jack-in-the-boxes, model people or cars which move along grooves or tracks, and seesaws. (The useful reference books in the *Linkers* series are listed in References and resources on page 88.)

Linked ICT activities

Use the hants.gov, toypost, ryallsweb and vintagetoys websites to look at old and new toys and the materials they are made from. (See References and resources on page 89.) Print some of the pictures.

Using a child-friendly digital camera, ask the children to take photographs of modern toys from the collection. Discuss the materials they are made from. Using a writing program such as *Textease* or *Clicker* (see page 89), ask the children to make a list of the materials that their toy is made from. Display the list alongside the toys in the class toy museum.

Materials

Toys are made from many different materials.

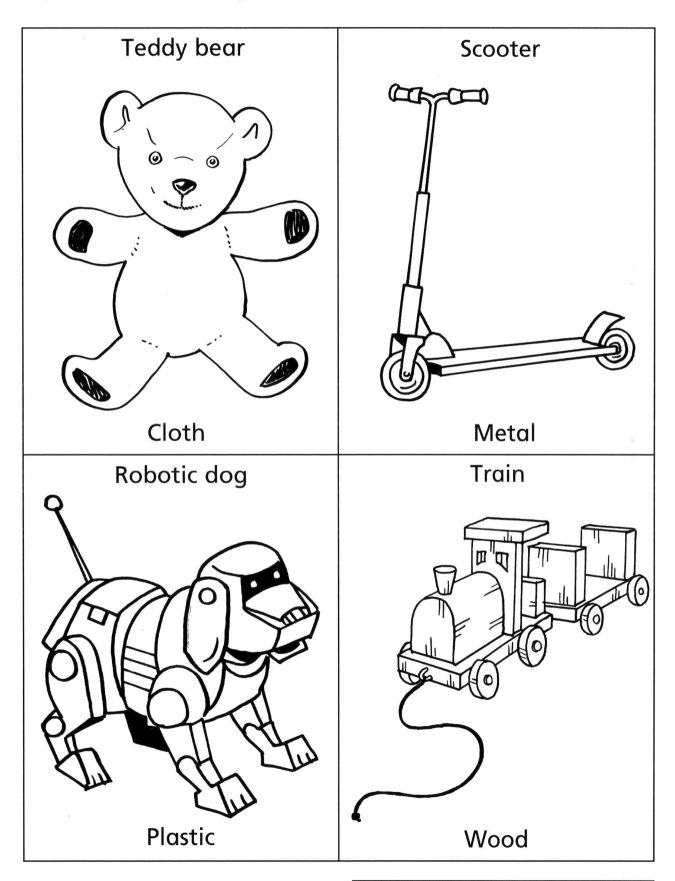

Teddy bear

Cloth

Scooter

Metal

Robotic dog

Plastic

Train

Wood

Materials

Draw a toy in the box.
Write a caption for your picture.

```




```

What is the toy made from? Tick the correct box. ✔

plastic ☐   metal ☐

cloth ☐   wood ☐

What colours are on it? Tick the correct boxes. ✔

black ☐   blue ☐   gold ☐

green ☐   red ☐   silver ☐

white ☐   yellow ☐

Name _____

Materials

Draw a toy in the box.
Write a caption for your picture.

_____

Write words to finish the sentences. Use the word bank to help you.

The toy is made from _____ .

The colours of the toy are _____

_____

```
                            WORD BANK
        black          metal          gold          wood
        cloth          blue           plastic       green
        red            silver         white         yellow
```

On the back of this sheet, draw three toys that could be made from metal.

Name _____

Materials

In the box draw a toy that can move.
Label each part and show what it is made from.
Use the word bank to help you.

WORD BANK

cloth   glass   metal   nylon   paper
plastic   rubber   wood

Write some sentences about why these are good materials for this toy.

_____

_____

_____

_____

Toys from the past: Roman to 1990s

Knucklebones (page 73)

This was a forerunner of 'fives'. It could be played by any number of players, who could have their own sets of knucklebones or they could take turns to use the same set. The playing pieces were the knucklebones of animals (usually sheep).

There were two main versions of this game:

1. On each turn the player placed the bones on the palm of their hand, tossed them into the air and tried to catch as many as possible on the back of the same hand. The player who caught the most was the winner.

2. In this version a small ball (usually made of leather or wood) was used as well as the five bones. One bone was placed on the ground and the ball was thrown into the air. The player had to pick up the bone on the ground and catch the ball before it landed. If successful, this was repeated with two bones, and so on up to five. The player who caught the greatest number of bones was the winner (in the case of a tie there would be a play-off).

Trigon (page 73)

Trigon was a game for three players. The players stood at the corners of a triangle whose sides were between four and seven metres long and threw a small hard ball to one another. Usually each player (*trigonalus*) had a score-keeper (*pilecripus*) standing by them, who counted the number of times the player caught the ball. Some sources say that the *pilecripus* counted the number of throws that were caught by the other players.

Pictures of people playing trigon have been found on the walls of Roman baths but there are different accounts of how it might have been played. A player threw or batted the ball to one of the others, who had to catch it and throw it or bat it to another player. Players could change the direction of play in order to surprise another player. Any catchable thrown or batted ball scored points. Sometimes more than one ball was used at once.

Hnefatafl (page 74)

This developed from a Roman game named *latrunculi* (brigands). It was played on a square board which could have 7, 9, 11, 13, 15 or 19 squares along each side. Hnefatafl boards have been found on the sites of many Norse settlements.

Hnefatafl was a game for two players. Different numbers of playing pieces were used, depending on the number of squares on the board. The player with the king had half as many pieces as their opponent.

Size of board	Dark pieces	Light pieces
7 x 7	12	6
9 x 9	16	8
11 x 11	24	12
13 x 13	24	12
15 x 15	32	16
19 x 19	48	24

The player with the king moved first. The king started on the central square. The object was to get the king into one of the corner squares. The other player had to try to trap the king. The pieces could move any number of squares along any unblocked straight vertical or horizontal lines. They could not jump over other pieces. To capture an opponent's piece a player had to trap it between two of their own pieces along any horizontal or vertical line. The king was trapped in the same way, but could not be captured (as in chess); also, as in chess, a player could win by trapping the king in this way, no matter how many other pieces were on the board.

Dice (page 75)

Dice have been found in excavations of ancient sites and have continued to be used up to the present day. As now, they were used for many types of game, to generate numbers.

Nine men's morris (page 75)

This is an ancient game, which was played by the ancient Egyptians and is still played. Nine men's morris boards have been uncovered during the excavation of several Anglo-Saxon and Norse sites. It was sometimes known as 'the other side of the board' and many boards for the game hnefatafl have been found which have a nine men's morris board on the reverse side.

It was a game for two players. They each started with nine pieces (each player had a different colour) which could be stones, shells, bones, pieces of wood and so on. Players took turns to place a piece on the board. Pieces could be placed anywhere two lines met. If a player managed to form a line of three pieces they could take one of their opponent's pieces off the board.

Once all the pieces were on the board, the players took turns to move a piece from one intersection to another adjacent one. The aim was to make a line of three (and thus have the right to remove one of the other player's pieces). To win the game, players had to remove all their opponent's pieces.

Tabula (page 75)

This game developed from a Roman game (also called *duodecim scripta* or *alea*). The exact rules are not known but it is thought to have been rather like backgammon. It was a game for two players and it is thought that each player started with 15 playing pieces. They took turns to roll three dice and to move their playing pieces around the board in an anti-clockwise direction. The winner was the first to move all 15 pieces around the board.

At the start of the game the pieces were placed off the board; to begin, the players rolled the dice.

Players could choose which pieces to move. They had to use the full value of all the dice they rolled unless all their moves were blocked by their opponent's pieces; in that case the remaining value could be used by their opponent to move their pieces.

A player could not place any pieces on a bar on which there were two of the other player's counters. A player could place a piece on a bar occupied by one of the other player's pieces; that piece was captured and had to go back to the start.

Blind man's buff (page 76)

This game dates from ancient times, but it was popular in Tudor times and afterwards, until the 1960s. It was played by any number (within reason) in a confined space such as a room or yard. One player was blindfolded and turned around several times. The other players spread out around the playing area. The blindfolded player had to catch any player by touching them. If a player was caught, that player became the catcher.

In one version of the game the blindfolded player had to identify the player who was caught by feeling their face. If they succeeded, the person identified was blindfolded. If not, the game continued with the same player blindfolded.

Cup and ball (page 76)

This was an individual game. To play, the ball was placed in the cup, the player held the handle of the cup, tossed the ball into the air and tried to catch it in the cup.

Hoop and stick (page 76)

This was played with a wooden or metal hoop (which was sometimes from a barrel – hoops held the staves of a barrel in place). The hoop was rolled along the ground and tapped with a stick to keep it rolling. Any straight stick could be used.

Masks (page 76)

Masks were used in the theatre in ancient times and their use continued for some types of play or mime. Children used masks for role-play; they enacted stories.

Roman toys

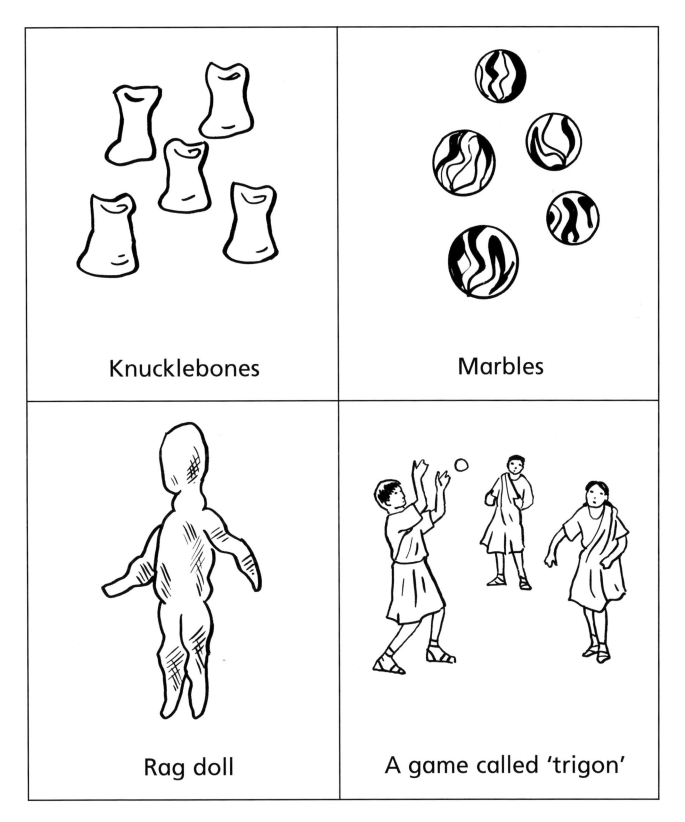

Knucklebones

Marbles

Rag doll

A game called 'trigon'

Norse toys

A board game called 'hnefatafl'

Boat (wood)

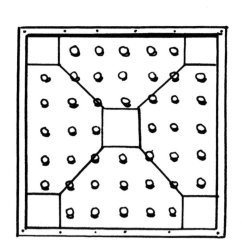

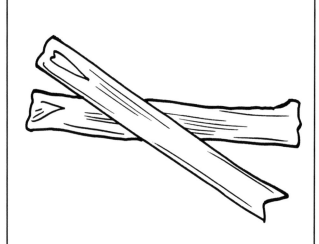

Ice skates (bone)

Chess pieces (walrus ivory)

Anglo-Saxon toys

Dice

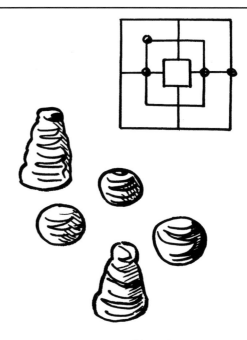

A game called 'nine men's morris'

Playing a game of tabula

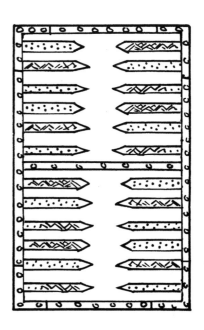

A game called 'tabula' (table)

Tudor toys

A game called 'blind man's buff'

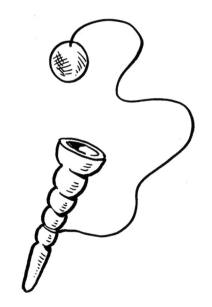

Cup and ball

Hoop and stick

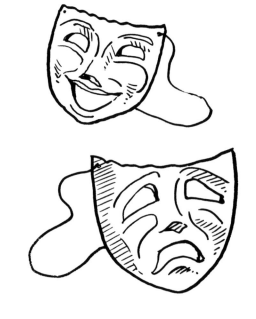

Masks

Victorian toys

Doll

Punch and Judy

Rocking horse

Theatre

1940s' toys

Fox puppet

Monkey

Spinning top

Truck

1950s' toys

Fire engine

Lenny the Lion

Racing car

Aeroplane

1960s' toys

Doll

Cooker

Frisbee

Joe 90 vehicle

1970s' toys

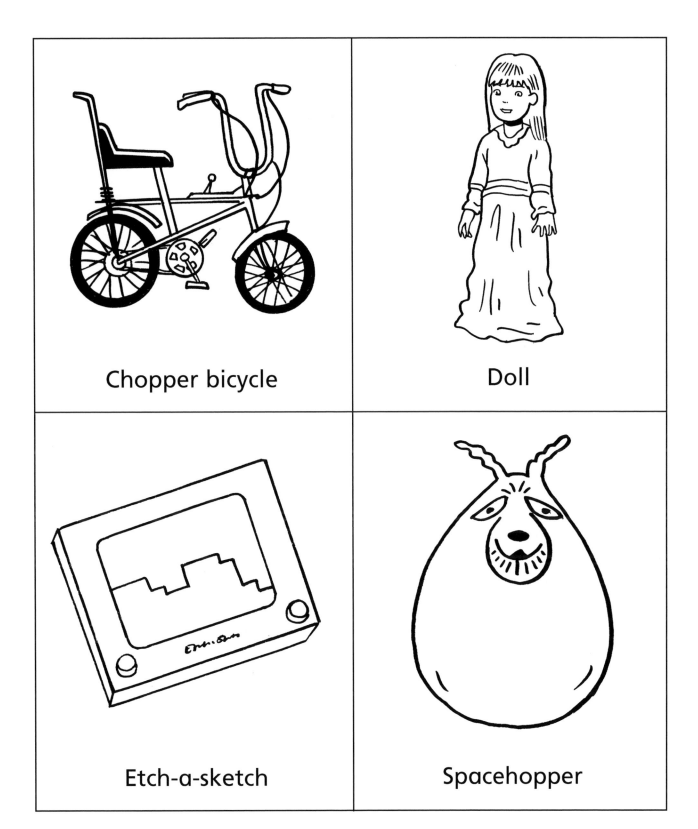

Chopper bicycle

Doll

Etch-a-sketch

Spacehopper

1980s' toys

Cabbage Patch doll

Rubik's cube

Smurf

Star Wars

1990s' toys

Doll

Motorbike

Mr Potato Head

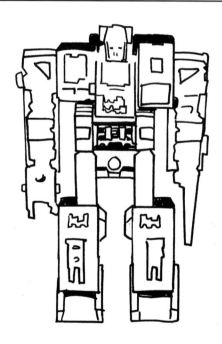

Transformer

Photocopiable word bank

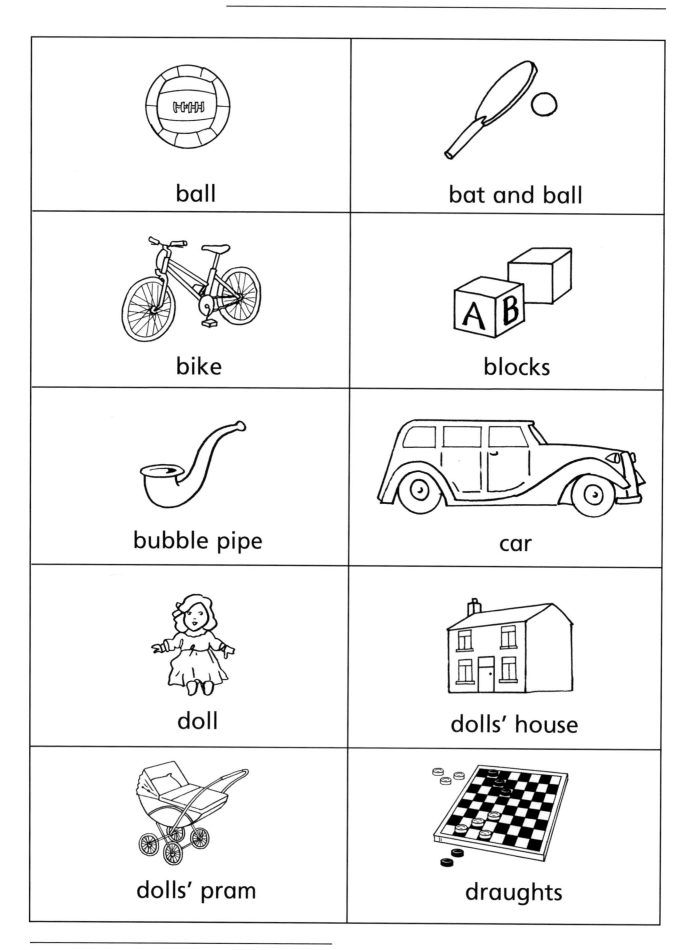

ball	bat and ball
bike	blocks
bubble pipe	car
doll	dolls' house
dolls' pram	draughts

Photocopiable word bank

drum

gramophone

hobbyhorse

hoop

horn

horse

jack-in-the-box

music box

penny whistle

racing car

Photocopiable word bank

record player	scooter
skates	skipping rope
snakes and ladders	teddy bears
top and whip	train
truck	yacht

Photocopiable word bank

ball	horse
bat and ball	jack-in-the-box
bike	music box
blocks	penny whistle
bubble pipe	racing car
car	record player
doll	scooter
dolls' house	skates
dolls' pram	skipping rope
draughts	snakes and ladders
drum	teddy bears
gramophone	top and whip
hobbyhorse	train
hoop	truck
horn	yacht

References and resources

Books for children

Hissey, J (1991) *Old Bear*. London: Red Fox.
Inkpen, M (1990) *Threadbare*. London: Hodder
Children's Book.
Linkers series:
Bryant-Mole, K (1996) *Toys discovered through Art
and Technology*. London: A & C Black.
Bryant-Mole, K (1996) *Toys discovered through
Geography*. London: A & C Black.
Bryant-Mole, K (1996) *Toys discovered through
History*. London: A & C Black.
Bryant-Mole, K (1996) *Toys discovered through Science*.
London: A & C Black.

Books for teachers

Goodfellow, C G (1998) *Dolls*. Princes Risborough:
Shire.
Pasierbska, H (1998) *Dolls' House Furniture*. Princes
Risborough: Shire.
Holdsworth, S, Crossley, J and Hardyment, C (1992)
*Innocence and Experience: Images of Children in British
Art From 1600 to the Present*. Manchester:
Manchester City Art Galleries.
Opie, J, Chilcott, D and Harris, J (1990) *The Letts
Guide to Collecting 20th-Century Toys*. London: Letts.
Marsh, M (2002) *Miller's Collectables*. London:
Octopus.
Stewart-Wilson, M (1988) *Queen Mary's Dolls' House*,
London: Bodley Head.
Cockrill, P (2001) *Teddy Bears and Soft Toys*. Princes
Risborough: Shire.

Websites

Early Learning Centre:
www.elc.co.uk
Information about toy music boxes:
http://pages.tias.com/1692/PictPage/1428229.html
*Information about other musical toys and record
players:*
www.misty.com/people/penny
www.hfmgv.org (click on Explore and learn, then
Collections)
Information about teddy bears:
www.historychannel.com/exhibits/toys/teddy.html
Barbie dolls:
www.dolls4play.com
Tiny Tears dolls:
www.dollinfo.com

Corgi cars:
www.corgi.co.uk
*100 years of toys (British Association of Toy
Manufacturers):*
www.batr.co.uk/batr2k

Museums

Museum of Childhood, Cambridge Heath Road,
Bethnal Green, London E2 9PA, Tel 020 8980 2415,
Fax 0208 983 5225; www.vam.ac.uk/vastatic/nmc/
Museum of Childhood, 42 High Street,
Edinburgh EH1 1TG, Tel 0131 529 4142/4119, Fax
0131 558 3103
Highland Museum of Childhood, The Old
Station, Strathpeffer, Ross and Cromarty IV14
9DH,
Tel 01997 421031, email:
info@hmoc.freeserve.co.uk;
www.hmoc.freeserve.co.uk
Museum of Childhood Memories, 1 Castle
Street, Beaumaris, Anglesey LL58 8AP, Tel 01248
712498; www.aboutbritain.com/museumof
childhoodmemories.htm
National Trust Museum of Childhood, Sudbury
Hall, Sudbury, Derbyshire DE6 5HT, Tel 01283 585
305;
www.aboutbritain.com/nationaltrustmuseumofchild
hood.htm
Windsor Castle (Queen Mary's Dolls' House),
The Visitor Office, Windsor Castle, Windsor,
Berkshire SL4 1NJ, Tel 0207 321 2233, Fax 0207
930 962, email:
information@royalcollection.org.uk;
www.royal.gov.uk/output/page576.asp

Toys in art (chapters 4 and 7)

Holdsworth, S, Crossley, J and Hardyment, C (1992)
*Innocence and Experience: Images of Children in British
Art From 1600 to the Present*. Manchester:
Manchester City Art Galleries. (includes most of the
paintings mentioned)

Postcard copies of Millais' 'Bubbles' may be
obtained from: Port Sunlight Heritage Centre, 95
Greendale Road, Port Sunlight CH62 4XE, Tel
0151 644 6466

Digital images of some of the paintings:
Breughel's 'Children's Games':

www.khm.at/homeE/homeE
Crane and Houghton's 'The Lowther Arcade':
www.bridgeman.co.uk (image ID: CRA 44023)
Dawson Watson's 'Bubbles':
www.bridgeman.co.uk **(image ID: CEC 44182)**
Ford Madox Brown's 'The English Boy':
www.bridgeman.co.uk (image ID: MAN 62932)
Hogarth's 'The Graham Children':
www.bridgeman.co.uk (image ID: BAL 5539)
Millais' 'Bubbles':
www.zona-pellucida.com/millais2.html
Van Somer's 'Child with a Rattle':
www.bridgeman.co.uk (image ID: LMG 109253)
Zoffany's 'John, Lord Willoughby de Broke and his
family': **www.getty.edu/art/collections/
objects/o110330.html**

Other paintings of toys in history to be found
at **www.bridgeman.co.uk**:
'Christmas Night' (Ramon Bayeu y Subias,
1746–93) image ID: JAL 109921
'The Toy Seller' (Augustus Bouvier, 1879) image ID:
PFA 185065
'The Happy Family' (Andre Dargelas, 1828–1906)
image ID: WAG 13326
'Children Dreaming of Toys' (Lizzie Mack, 1886)
image ID: BAL 8407
'Painted Tin Penny Toys' (German School, 1890)
image ID: MOL 1511

Resources recommended for linked ICT activities

Software:
All About Toys Granada Learning/SEMERC,
Granada Television, Quay Street, Manchester M60
9EA, Tel 0161 827 2927
Clicker 4 Crick Software, 35 Charter Gate,
Quarry Park Close, Moulton Park, Northampton
NN3 6QB, Tel 01604 671 691; www.cricksoft.com

Counter for Windows Granada Learning/
SEMERC, Granada Television, Quay Street,
Manchester M60 9EA, Tel 0161 827 2927
Dazzle Granada Learning/SEMERC, Granada
Television, Quay Street, Manchester M60 9EA, Tel
0161 827 2927
Musical Leaps and Bounds and **Beetles** REM
(Rickett Educational Media Ltd), Great Western
House, Langport, Somerset TA10 9YU; Tel 01458
254 700
My World for Windows Granada Learning/
SEMERC, Granada Television, Quay Street,
Manchester M60 9EA, Tel 0161 827 2927
Textease 2000 Softease Ltd, Market Place,
Ashbourne, Derbyshire DE6 1ES, Tel 01335 343
421, Fax 01335 343 422; www.softease.com

Websites:
www.dollshouseshop.com
www.hants.gov.uk/museum/toys (good
selection of toys made from different materials)
www.honeytoys.co.uk
www.oldbear.co.uk
www.pollocksweb.co.uk (Pollocks toy museum
and toyshop)
www.ryallsweb.freeserve.co.uk (old tin plate
toys)
www.teddymatters.com
www.toymuseum.co.uk
www.toypost.co.uk/pages/toys2.html (replica
wooden toys)
www.vintagetoys.co.uk (metal toy trains)

Digital camera:
Digital Dream 'L'Elegante' digital camera for
children: TAG Learning, Tel 01474 357 350, Fax
01474 537 887; www.taglearning.co.uk